"Given all that has been written on the subject it is surprising to find a volume with so much that is fresh, new, and challenging. Naomi Lynn has done well in assembling these diverse perspectives on women and the Constitution."
J. Darcy, PhD, Professor, Department of Political Science, Oklahoma State University, Stillwater, Oklahoma

"Span[s] the history of the constitution, beginning with consideration of an early female writer and patriot, Mercy Otis Warren, and ending with an analysis of contemporary amendments to state constitutions. Several of the essays which deal with historical questions provide new insights into the tension between women's demands for rights and other political forces in the society. Locke's essay on the exclusion of African-American women from voting rights in the post-Civil War era and McDonagh's analysis of Congressional voting on suffrage in the progressive era both strip way myths associated with the women's movement. O'Connor and Segal's essay on the impact of Sandra Day O'Connor's appointment to the Supreme Court demonstrates that her 'swing' position has, in fact, moved the court to a more pro-feminist stance in some cases. Finally, the excellent essays by Mezey and Rhode establish a debate on possible ways for the courts to approach gender-based legislation. In summary, the essays in this collection are diverse, well-argued, and accessible enough to provide excellent supplementary reading for courses addressing gender issues."
Barbara Bardes, PhD, Dean, University College, Loyola University, Chicago, Illinois

"This book presents a range of interesting essays covering topics of both historical and legal interest. The authors of these [chapters] bring a range of skills and new perspectives to important issues. Significant new research is presented as are new analyses of major legal trends."
Marjorie F. Knowles, LLB, AB, Dean, College of Law, Georgia State University, Atlanta, Georgia

"This is a useful collection of historical, empirical, and theoretical essays on women and constitutions—state and federal—in the United States. The methodological and topical diversity of the essays testifies to the contemporary richness of the two genres intersecting in this volume: women's studies and constitutional studies. Med's and Rhode's essays on feminist jurisprudence are provocative; Locke's constitutional history read through African-American women's experience is sobering; the essays on women and state constitutions open a new domain for thinking about women and political change."
Wendy Brown, PhD, Associate Professor, Women's Studies and History of Consciousness, and Director, Feminist Studies Focused Research Activity, University of California at Santa Cruz

Women, Politics and the Constitution

Women, Politics and the Constitution

Naomi B. Lynn
Editor

Women, Politics and the Constitution was simultaneously issued by The Haworth Press, Inc. under the same title, as a special issue of *Women & Politics,* Volume 10, Number 2 1990, Rita Mae Kelly, Editor.

Harrington Park Press
New York • London

0-918393-75-2

Published by

Harrington Park Press, 10 Alice Street, Binghamton, NY 13904-1580
EUROSPAN/Harrington, 3 Henrietta Street, London WC2E 8LU England

Harrington Park Press is a subsidiary of The Haworth Press, Inc., 10 Alice Street, Binghamton, New York 13904-1580.

Women, Politics and the Constitution was originally published as *Women & Politics*, Volume 10, Number 2 1990.

Cover design by Marshall Andrews.

Library of Congress Cataloging-in-Publication Data

Women, Politics and the Constitution / Naomi B. Lynn, editor.
p. cm.
Selection of papers from a conference held in Atlanta, Ga., Feb. 1988, sponsored by the Carter Center of Emory University, the Jimmy Carter Library, and Georgia State University.
Also published as v. 10, no. 2 of Women & politics.
Includes bibliographical references.
ISBN 0-918393-75-2 (acid free paper)
1. Women – Legal status, laws, etc. – United States – History – Congresses. 2. United States – Constitutional history – Congresses. 3. Women – United States – Social conditions – Congresses. I. Lynn, Naomi B. II. Emory University. Carter Center. III. Jimmy Carter Library. IV. Georgia State University.
KF478.A5W63 1990b
342.73'0878 – dc20
[347.302878] 90-37948
CIP

For Janice Mendenhall Regenstein

ABOUT THE EDITOR

Naomi B. Lynn, PhD, is Dean of the College of Public and Urban Affairs, and Professor of Public Administration and Political Science at Georgia State University in Atlanta. She is past National President of the American Society for Public Administration, past National President of the Women's Caucus for Political Science, and has served on the Executive Council of the American Political Science Association. Currently, she is on the editorial boards of *Women & Politics* and the *Journal of Politics.*

Dr. Lynn has contributed chapters to several books including *Women Leaders in Contemporary U.S. Politics* (Lynn Rienner Publishers, 1987), *A Portrait of Marginality: The Political Behavior of the American Woman* (John Wiley & Sons, Inc., 1974) and *United Nations Decade for Women World Conference* (The Haworth Press, 1984) of which she was the editor. She also has had articles published in numerous political science and public administration journals.

CONTENTS

About the Contributors

Irwin N. Gertzog teaches political science at Allegheny College and offers courses on the U.S. Congress, the Presidency, and Women and Politics. He is the author of, among other works, *Congressional Women: Their Recruitment, Treatment and Behavior* (1984) and is currently preparing a comprehensive study of female suffrage in New Jersey from 1790 to 1807.

Judith J. Lane is a recent honors graduate of Shenandoah College and Conservatory, where she majored in English. She is actively engaged in community and church work and has recently accepted employment outside the home as an office manager.

Larry M. Lane is a member of the adjunct faculty of The American University and of Virginia Tech. His principal areas of interest are human resource management and administrative processes. He served in the federal service for 30 years and now writes and lectures on issues concerning the public service.

Mamie E. Locke is Associate Professor of Political Science at Hampton University. Her research and publications are concentrated in the area of black women's issues, particularly cross-cultural analyses and the intersection of sex, race, and class. She is currently writing articles on Fannie Lou Hamer and womanist theory.

Naomi B. Lynn is Dean of the College of Public and Urban Affairs at Georgia State University. She is past president of The American Society for Public Administration, has served on the executive councils of the American Political Science Association and The National Association of Schools of Public Affairs and Administration, and has been National President of The Women's Caucus for Political Science. In 1986, she was elected a fellow of The National

Academy of Public Administration. Dr. Lynn is the author of numerous articles and books in the fields of public administration, political science, and women and politics.

Susan A. MacManus is Professor of Public Administration and Political Science at the University of South Florida, Tampa. She is the author of numerous books and articles on the impact of public policy on women and minorities. While on the faculty of the University of Houston, Professor MacManus served during an eight-year period as President of the Houston Area Women's Center and as Vice President of Finance, Treasurer, and member of the Board of Directors.

Eileen Lorenzi McDonagh is currently National Science Foundation Visiting Professor at the Henry A. Murray Research Center, Radcliffe College, and Associate Professor of Political Science at Northeastern University. Her NSF-funded research project investigates the constituency influence of grass-roots referenda votes upon subsequent voting in the House of Representatives on social welfare, civil rights, and government management issues in the Progressive Era decades of 1900 to 1920.

Susan Gluck Mezey is Associate Professor of Political Science at Loyola University of Chicago. She hold a PhD from Syracuse University and a law degree from De Paul University. She does research on the policy-making role of federal courts and has published a book entitled *No Longer Disabled: The Federal Courts and the Politics of Social Security Disability*.

Karen O'Connor is Professor of Political Science and Adjunct Professor of Law at Emory University. She is the author of numerous articles and books on women and the law and the role of interest groups in the judicial process.

Sandra Day O'Connor has been Justice of the U.S. Supreme Court since 1981, the first women ever to serve in that capacity. She served on the Arizona Court of Appeals from 1979 to 1981, and from 1975 to 1979 she was Superior Court Judge in Maricopa County, Arizona. Justice O'Connor has also held legislative office as an Arizona state senator from 1969 to 1975, during which time she chaired the State, County, and Municipal Affairs Committee and served on the Arizona Advisory Council on Intergovernmental Relations. She graduated *magna cum laude* from Stanford University in 1950 and was awarded an LLB from that institution in 1952.

Deborah L. Rhode is Professor of Law and Director of the Institute for Research on Women and Gender at Stanford Unviersity. She received her BA from Yale College, *summa cum laude*, Phi Beta Kappa, and her Juris Doctor from Yale Law School. After clerking for Justice Thurgood Marshall on the Supreme Court, she joined the Stanford Faculty. Her teaching and research focuses on legal ethics and gender discrimination. Her publications include *Gender and Justice* (Harvard University Press, 1989) and *Theoretical Perspectives on Sexual Difference* (Yale Press, 1990), an edited collection.

Jeffrey A. Segal is Associate Professor of Political Science at State University of New York at Stony Brook. He is the author of numerous articles on judicial behavior that have appeared in journals including the *American Political Science Review* and the *Journal of Politics* among others.

Introduction

In February 1988, a conference was held in Atlanta, Georgia, to commemorate, recognize, debate, and discuss the significance of the U.S. Constitution on women's history, rights, and present status. *Women and the Constitution: A Bicentennial Perspective* was sponsored by the Carter Center of Emory University, the Jimmy Carter Library, and Georgia State University. A great deal of the credit for this meeting goes to Rosalyn Carter, who recognized its importance and invited Former First Ladies Lady Bird Johnson, Betty Ford, and Pat Nixon to serve as coconveners, and whose sponsorship, influence, work, and leadership contributed greatly to its success.

For those who were fortunate enough to attend, the Atlanta meeting was an "experience" rather than a conference. Women and men from 50 states and 10 foreign countries came together to discuss our past, assess our current status, and predict and plan our future. These 1500 attendees were joined by many individuals who are playing or have played an active and critical role both in interpreting and in determining the constitutional status of women. Among those participating were Justice Sandra Day O'Connor, Barbara Jordan, Geraldine Ferraro, Coretta Scott King, Olympia Snow, Bella Abzug, and other legal and academic leaders. All speeches and papers from the conference are stored in the National Archives and will be our legacy to the next generation of scholars.

The papers that have been chosen for inclusion in this volume were selected from those that seemed most suitable for the *Women & Politics* journal and were all anonymously reviewed. The Carter Center of Emory University is presently preparing a multivolume set of curriculum materials that will be available in the spring of 1990.

It is most appropriate to begin this issue with the address delivered by Justice Sandra Day O'Connor, the first woman to be appointed to the U.S. Supreme Court.

Karen O'Connor and Jeffrey Segal in their paper, "Justice Sandra Day O'Connor and the Supreme Court's Reaction to Its First Female Member," conclude that Justice O'Connor's appointment to the Supreme Court had a positive impact on gender-related cases and that the Court became more receptive to sex discrimination claims after she joined her male colleagues.

Although it is true that women were invisible during the Constitutional Convention, it is also true that some women participated in the intellectual discussion that provided the political and philosophical justification for the establishment of our nation. Historians have yet to determine the extent of their influence. Judith and Larry Lane write about one significant participant, Mercy Otis Warren.

If all women were invisible during the Convention, certainly Afro-American women would have the strongest claim to that dubious distinction. Mamie Locke's paper supports this contention as she discusses how Afro-American women were diminished from three-fifths of a person in the original Constitution to zero status after the passage of the Fifteenth Amendment.

In her article, "The Significance of the Nineteenth Amendment: A New Look at Civil Rights, Social Welfare, and Woman Suffrage Alignments in the Progressive Era," Eileen McDonagh demonstrates how women's nineteenth-century activity was the prototype for current political activity. Her article is also an excellent example of how current research on women is resulting in needed revisionism and in a deeper understanding of historical events and interpretations. For example, McDonagh challenges the premise that the women's suffrage movement was negatively tied to civil rights for Afro-Americans and new immigrants. The rhetoric to gain the vote took advantage of contemporary prejudices, but McDonagh demonstrates that within Congress there was no correlation between the vote for women's suffrage and the votes limiting electoral rights for other groups. The vote for women's suffrage was the only positive civil rights issue passed during the Progressive Era, but it was not at the expense of other marginal groups.

Women received the vote for many different reasons. Irwin Gertzog explains that, in New Jersey, women voted during the post-

Revolution period because they had become the beneficiaries of a struggle for economic and social power. Those who exercised this right were motivated by the same forces that determined male participation. Unfortunately, they were unable to mobilize the political strength to protect their rights from efforts to guarantee white male political dominance.

Susan Gluck Mezey's paper argues that gender should receive the same legal scrutiny and review as is currently applied to race and that preferential treatment for pregnancy is as legitimate as other compensatory racial legislation. Regrettably, recent Supreme Court cases have weakened racial standards for scrutiny and will probably make it even more difficult for gender-based cases to receive favorable decisions.

Whereas Mezey concludes that preferential treatment during pregnancy is essential if women are to achieve workplace equality, a different perspective is presented by Deborah Rhode. Rhode examines court decisions that have placed women at a disadvantage; in this discussion are decisions that claim to be protective of women but that have in fact supported sex stereotypes and the continuation of gender-based inequality. In her review of issues related to pregnancy, Rhode concludes that "Mommy tracks" can become "Mommy traps" and are not likely to serve women's long-term interests. She prefers a legal approach that would require not just equal treatment of women, but the *treatment of women as equals*.

In a review of state constitutional changes between 1977 and 1985, Susan MacManus finds little progress in the area of gender-related civil rights and liberties, but positive changes in economic and social policies related to women may be discerned.

I want to express my appreciation to all the reviewers who helped with this issue. I also want to thank Reggie Foster, who helped with all aspects of editing for this volume.

Naomi B. Lynn

Women and the Constitution: A Bicentennial Perspective

Sandra Day O'Connor

SUMMARY. This paper provides an overview of the history of women and the U.S. Constitution. It highlights the exclusion of women from most political and economic protections provided men. The critical role of the application of the Equal Protection Clause to women from 1971 to the 1990s is stressed. The importance of the interpretations of the U.S. Supreme Court Justices for women is made evident.

This is a very special event. The bicentennial of our Constitution has been the subject of more than a year of celebrations and observances. It has produced some dramatic changes for me and for my colleagues on the Supreme Court. It was in order to prepare for the 200th anniversary of our national charter that Chief Justice Warren Burger stepped down. One of my colleagues and a former Arizonan, William Rehnquist, has become our sixteenth Chief Justice. Antonin Scalia, a former Court of Appeals Judge, has joined us, and we are also joined by Court of Appeals Judge Anthony Kennedy.

It seems natural for Supreme Court Justices to be enthusiastic about the bicentennial of the document we spend so many of our waking hours thinking and arguing about—and so many pages of the *United States Reports* writing about. But it is perhaps not so common today for people to examine our Constitution. Although

---

Sandra Day O'Connor is Associate Justice, Supreme Court of the United States.

This paper was published by the Carter Center of Emory University in a pamphlet containing several of the speeches that were presented at the *Women and the Constitution* Symposium. It is reprinted here with permission of the Carter Center.

200 years ago most Americans debated the merits of the proposed Constitution, recent polls indicate that today almost half of our citizens do not know why the Constitution was drafted, nor even what is meant by the Bill of Rights; 75% erroneously believe that the Constitution guarantees a free public education; 49% erroneously believe that the President can suspend the Constitution in time of national emergency; and 64% believe that the Constitution establishes English as our national language. I dare say an even higher percentage have little or no understanding of how the Constitution and the Bill of Rights apply to women.

With such widespread lack of understanding about our nation's charter, the bicentennial celebration has been welcome indeed. It provides an opportunity for each of us to learn more about the ideas embodied in the Constitution and the ways in which those ideas shape our lives. It is not enough simply to read the document; we need to learn how the Constitution has been interpreted and applied in the courts of this land in order to understand what it has come to mean at the end of the twentieth century. This symposium gives us an opportunity to review one particular area of constitutional law—specifically, its application to women.

One reason the Constitution and the Bill of Rights have survived for two centuries is that, for the most part, they were drafted in intentionally broad and general terms. The drafters left to future generations the task of giving their words texture and meaning in the context of changing times and current problems. Although the power of judicial review is said by some to be the cornerstone of our constitutional law, courts are almost never the first to ponder the constitutional questions that come before them. Article III of the Constitution empowers federal courts to decide only genuine cases or controversies. This means that in the first instance it is up to state and federal legislators and executives to decide whether the laws they enact or the actions they undertake are constitutional. Many provisions of the Constitution are addressed directly to legislators and executive officials. And even when the government acts, the judiciary does not come into play until someone with a personal stake in the matter challenges the government action or practice in court.

The point is that the Supreme Court almost never has the first word in interpreting the Constitution. The Court is a uniquely reactive institution. Our agenda is shaped by the issues and concerns of the nation as a whole. Almost every political, economic, and social problem and change in our society has a way of finding its way eventually to the Court's marble halls. But we cannot just pluck interesting issues out of the air and decide them for the benefit of future generations. When the Court's agenda changes, as it surely did beginning in 1970 in the area of sex discrimination, the change is most frequently a delayed response to changes in the nation's agenda. It is dictated by external forces—the actions of the other branches of government, the decisions of the lower courts, and ultimately the concerns of the public. The Court is only rarely in the forefront of establishing new major legal standards, and its articulation of principles of social policy has typically been within the bounds of general public perceptions at the time. The story of women and the Constitution is illustrative.

Abigail Adams advised her husband in 1776 to "remember the Ladies" in drafting the new nation's charter. Women, she said, "would not hold [themselves] bound by any laws in which [they] have no voice or representation" (Anthony 1958, 102). Her advice had little effect on her husband, John. He answered that men would not give up their masculine systems, but they would be fair, because in practice men "were the subjects" of their wives (Norton 1980, 163). His response reflected a view of women sometimes expressed both in England and in the Colonies. It is reminiscent of the words of Samuel Johnson, the English author and conversationalist, who once told a friend, "Nature has given women so much power that the law has very wisely given them little" (McNamara 1967, 571).

As we all know, the Constitution ratified in Philadelphia on September 17, 1787, was produced and voted upon by 55 delegates—all men. The final draft contains no specific mention of women, although at various places throughout the document the faultlessly gender-neutral terms "person" and "citizen" are used. The Great Compromise—providing for representation in the House of Representatives on the basis of population, and representation in the Senate on the basis of two representatives from each state—made it possible for the Constitutional Convention to produce ultimate agreement on our national charter. There was, as far as we know, no disagreement that representation in Congress should be based on the whole free population, women as well as men. The only express reference to this of which I am aware was in Resolution 7, submitted by Edmund Randolph of Virginia on June 28, which "resolved that the right of suffrage in the first branch of the legislature of the United States ought to be in proportion to the whole number of white and other free citizens and inhabitants of every age, sex, and condition including those bound to servitude for a term of years and three-fifths of all other persons not comprehended in the foregoing description except Indians not paying their taxes in each state." The Committee on Style rephrased this language as part of Article 1, Section 2, referring simply to "free persons."

The Constitution, however, left the regulation and qualification of voters to be determined by each state. In 1787, only the state of New Jersey permitted women to vote, although that privilege was removed in 1807 because of controversy surrounding a particular election in Elizabethtown. It was not to be extended again to women by any state until Wyoming did so in 1869, perhaps partly with tongue in cheek. And it was not until the addition of the Nineteenth Amendment in the early part of this century that the federal Constitution guaranteed all citizens the right to vote.

The ratification of the Bill of Rights in 1791 had little immediate effect on the legal status or rights of women. Its strictures were limited initially to the federal government; the states were free to continue as before in fashioning the political and legal rights of their citizens. State legislation affecting women was drawn primarily from the British common law. Only in the case of unmarried women were the laws in this country somewhat more generous than those in England, at least insofar as property ownership and management were concerned.

It was not until after the Civil War and the resultant adoption of the Thirteenth, Fourteenth, and Fifteenth Amendments to our Constitution that there were arguably some national guaranties for certain individual liberties, which the states could not abridge. But even these additions to our Constitution did not easily translate into concepts that benefitted women as a group until the last half of the twentieth century. Until that time, despite the efforts of women such as Elizabeth Cady Stanton, Susan B. Anthony, and Sojourner Truth, society as a whole generally accepted the separate and unequal status of women.

The Fourteenth Amendment prohibits states from "denying to any person . . . the equal protection of the laws." There is little evidence to suggest that, at the time of its adoption in 1868, this Amendment was seen as a vehicle of women's equality under law. In fact, the Fourteenth Amendment introduced sex-specific language into the Constitution: Section 2 of the Amendment, which dealt with legislative representation and voting, said that if the right to vote were "denied to any of the *male* inhabitants" of a state aged 21 or over [italics mine] then the proportional representation in that state would be reduced accordingly. Moreover, the Supreme Court determined in 1872, in the *Slaughter-House Cases*, that the Equal Protection Clause should be narrowly interpreted to apply only to state laws that discriminated against blacks. Justice Miller, speaking for the Court, said, "We doubt very much whether any action by a state not directed by way of discrimination against the Negroes as a class . . . will *ever* be held to come within the purview of [the Equal Protection Clause]" (*Slaughter-House Cases* 1872, 81).

The same Court on the very next day handed down the decision denying Myra Bradwell's claim that the State of Illinois had denied her the privileges and immunities of United States citizenship when it refused, because of her sex, to give her a license to practice law (*Bradwell v. Illinois* 1872). The Court's holding was that the right to practice law in a state was not a federal privilege, but the concurring opinion of Justice Bradley reflected the nineteenth-century view of the separate and unequal status of women: As he put it, their "natural and proper timidity and delicacy . . . unfits [them] for many of the occupations of civil life" (141 [Bradley, concurring]).

Two years later the Court refused to sustain the claim of Virginia Minor that Missouri's male-only voting laws were unconstitutional under the Fourteenth Amendment (*Minor v. Happersett* 1874). The Court unanimously held that the Constitution did not confer the right of suffrage on anyone, and it noted that none of the new states that had been admitted to the Union had conferred that right upon women.

In 1880 the Court upheld a West Virginia law restricting jury service to men (*Strauder v. West Virginia*), a decision that was not overturned until 1975 (*Taylor v. Louisiana*). Indeed, the practice of restricting jury service to men unless women registered separately to serve as jurors was upheld as late as 1961. That case came to the Court from Florida, where an all-male jury had convicted Gwendolyn Hoyt of murdering her husband with a baseball bat. Her defense was that his marital infidelity had so enraged her that she had killed him in a fit of temporary insanity. She argued that the effect of Florida's system of jury registration by women had the effect of unconstitutionally depriving her of a jury of her peers. In upholding Florida's jury practices, the Court said, "Despite the enlightened emancipation of women from the restrictions and protections of bygone years, and their entry into many parts of community life formerly considered to be reserved to men, woman is still regarded as the center of the home and family life" (*Hoyt v. Florida* 1961, 61-62). So stating, the Court upheld the blanket excuse of all women from jury service.

It was not until after World War I and the unrelenting efforts of the Suffragettes that the Nineteenth Amendment was adopted in 1920, finally giving women the right to vote. But even the tremendous gain of the franchise did not result in serious demands for equality in laws relating to women in the labor force. The Federal Women's Bureau, Labor Secretary Frances Perkins, and Eleanor Roosevelt, among others, opposed the first introduction of an Equal Rights Amendment, and they supported laws giving women special protection such as maximum working hours. Such a law had been upheld by the Supreme Court in 1908 in *Muller v. Oregon*, where the Court had said, "History discloses the fact that woman has always been dependent upon man. . . . She is properly placed in a class by herself, and legislation designed for her protection may be sustained, even when like legislation is not necessary for men" (*Muller v. Oregon* 1908, 421, 422). The Court reasoned that protectionist legislation was justified because it was designed to compensate for the special burdens resting on women.

Upon reading the Court's opinion it is apparent that many of the "burdens" the Court perceived were the result of societal stereotypes rather than actual biological differences between the sexes. The Court found, for example, that the two sexes differed in "the self-reliance that enables one to assert full rights, and in the capacity to maintain the struggle for subsistence" (422). Yet one sees even in that opinion an awkward attempt by the Court to come to grips with the problem of how physical differences between the sexes should affect their treatment under the law, a problem that has continued to perplex the courts in the succeeding years.

For the first half of the twentieth century, the Court continued to defer to legislative judgments regarding the differences between the sexes. In 1948, Valentine Goesaert and three other women challenged the constitutionality of a Michigan statute forbidding a woman from being a bartender unless she was "the wife or daughter of the male owner" of the bar. The Court, in an opinion by Justice Frankfurter, rejected the claim that the statute violated the Equal Protection Clause, saying that "despite the vast changes in the social and legal position of women," the state unquestionably could forbid all women from working as bartenders. The Court was unwilling to second-guess the judgment of the Michigan legislature that bar ownership was hazardous to women (*Goesaert v. Cleary* 1948, 465, 466).

Until the latter half of this century, few women considered practicing law or medicine or any of the other traditionally male occupations. In family law, property law, and elsewhere, women—particularly black women—were relegated to a position that could be described at best as second class. Correctly perceiving the law as an engine of oppression, few women were eager to get on the train.

Happily, the last half of this century has witnessed a revolution in women's legal and political status. My chambers window in Washington, D.C., commands a view of a small brick house, the headquarters of the National Women's Party and the home of suffragist Alice Paul. It serves as a daily reminder to me that less than 70 years ago women had yet to obtain that most basic civil right, the right to vote. It also serves as a reminder that single-minded determination and effort can bring about fundamental changes in even a well-entrenched system of discrimination.

The great catalyst for the growth of civil rights litigation generally was the school desegregation case of *Brown v. Board of Education* decided in 1954. In the aftermath of that landmark decision, public and legislative attention began to focus not only on racial discrimination but also on sex-based discrimination. Women emerged in significant numbers all across the country in the 1960s to demand equal opportunity, primarily in the work force. Pursuant to its power under the Commerce Clause, Congress enacted both the Equal Pay Act of 1963 and Title VII of the Civil Rights Act of 1964, prohibiting employment discrimination on the basis of race or sex. In 1972, Congress sent the proposed Equal Rights Amendment to the states for ratification; in response, although it was not ratified, many states became active in reviewing state legislation to remove discriminatory laws and to pass state civil rights legislation.

The Supreme Court began to look more closely at legislation providing dissimilar treatment for similarly situated women and men in the early 1970s. The first case in which the Court found a state law discriminating against women to be unconstitutional was *Reed v. Reed* (1971). The case was decided more than 100 years after the ratification of the Fourteenth Amendment. Applying only a rationality standard, the Court struck down an Idaho law giving men an automatic preference in appointments as administrators of estates. Following *Reed*, the Court invalidated a broad range of discriminatory statutes under the Equal Protection Clause of the Fourteenth Amendment: for example, a federal law providing for determination of a spouse's dependency based on the sex of the member of the armed forces claiming the benefits (*Frontiero v. Richardson* 1973), a Social Security Act provision allowing widows but not widowers to collect survivors benefits (*Weinberger v. Wiesenfeld* 1975), a state law requiring divorced fathers to support their sons until age 21 but their daughters only to age 18 (*Stanton v. Stanton* 1975), a state law permitting the sale of beer to women at age 18 but not to men until age 21 (*Craig v. Boren* 1976), a state law requiring men but not women to pay alimony after divorce (*Orr v. Orr* 1979), and a state statute granting only husbands the right to manage and dispose of jointly owned property without the spouse's consent (*Kirchberg v. Feenstra* 1981). In 1976, in the case of *Craig v. Boren*, the Court adopted a somewhat stricter standard of review for sex-based classifications and held that to "withstand constitutional challenge [under the Equal Protection Clause] . . . classifications by gender must serve important governmental objectives and must be substantially related to achievement of those objectives" (1979, 197).

All in all, the Court has heard more than 50 cases since 1971 involving various sex-based challenges under the Equal Protection Clause to state and federal laws relating to hiring, promotions, maternity leave, disability insurance, pension rights, and seniority. Some of the challenges have been brought by women, some by men. Not all such challenges have been successful, yet there is no question but that the Court has now made clear that it will no longer view as benign archaic and stereotypic notions concerning the roles and abilities of males and females. A statute classifying people on the basis of sex will not be upheld absent an exceedingly persuasive justification for the classification.

The volume of cases in the Supreme Court dealing with sex discrimination has declined somewhat in the 1980s. Several of the more recent cases brought before the Court have involved interpretations of Title VII rather than of the Equal Protection Clause. In *Hishon v. King & Spalding* (1984), the Court held that, once a law firm makes partnership consideration a privilege of employment, the firm may not discriminate on the basis of sex in its selection of partners. The Court has also recognized that sexual harassment creating a hostile workplace environment violates Title VII (*Meritor Savings Bank, FSB v. Vinson* 1986). During the last term, the Court held that Title VII does not prohibit an employer from adopting an affirmative action plan taking sex into account in order to remedy the underrepresentation of women in traditionally segregated jobs (*Johnson v. Transportation Agency* 1987).

Other recent cases have involved First Amendment challenges to state and local laws designed to end sex discrimination. In *Roberts v. Jaycees* (1984), the Supreme Court upheld a Minnesota statute that required the Jaycees to admit women as full voting members. The Court upheld a recent California law requiring Rotary Clubs to admit women. The Court reasoned that any infringement on the club members' freedom of association was justified by the State's compelling interest in eliminating sex discrimination and in assuring women equal access to leadership skills and business contacts

(*Board of Directors of Rotary International v. Rotary Club of Duarte* 1987).

It has been 15 years since the Court's controversial ruling in *Roe v. Wade* (1973) invalidating state laws restricting abortions during the first three months of pregnancy. This decision, which is of enormous interest to women (whether they favor or oppose it), rested not on the Equal Protection Clause but on a right of privacy, which the Court held to be implicit in the Constitution. Since *Roe v. Wade*, the Court has heard approximately 14 additional cases dealing with the regulation and funding of abortion procedures.

There is no doubt that for the remainder of this century the federal and state courts will continue to see cases dealing with sex-based discrimination, affirmative action, reproductive rights, and other sensitive issues affecting women. As I have noted, the Court's response and the development of constitutional doctrine is typically a delayed response to changes and new developments in the nation's focus and agenda. The Court is not a bad place from which to get some sense of the nation's concerns, or at least its national legal concerns. The more than 4,000 petitions for review each year come from all across the country and involve a very wide range of legal issues. The Court hears oral argument in cases which have their genesis in front-page actions by Congress as well as in the actions of police officers in tiny towns. The attorneys who appear before the Court, and the clients whose problems have brought them there, present a similarly broad geographical cross-section.

E. B. White once said, "Democracy is based on the recurrent suspicion that more than half of the people are right more than half of the time" (Green 1982, 295). In the narrow view, the Supreme Court is based on the suspicion that five Justices are similarly correct. In the broader view, I think that the Justices contribute to the wider democracy. We struggle with national issues and attempt to define from national perspective what it is that the federal laws and the Constitution say. If you do not agree with all of the Court's holdings, you are certainly not alone. But you may be confident that we never stop trying, in our writings on every case on our agenda, to contribute appropriately to the fragile balances of our national democracy.

To put it differently, the Court is somewhat akin to a fire department. When Congress or the Executive Branch or an individual state lights a new fire, we are inevitably summoned to attend to the blaze. Some litigants will ask us to fan the flames, others will demand their extinguishment, and still others will request only that the fire not be allowed to spread. But, unlike most fire departments, justice moves slowly, so we usually arrive on the scene some years late. Once there, however, we usually must linger for a while. It often takes a series of decisions to flesh out a new statute, or to draw new boundaries between state and federal authority, or to reconsider the limits on government intrusions on individual rights. Eventually, of course, most of what can be done in an appellate court is completed, and thereafter we see little more of that particular conflagration. In the broad area of women and the Constitution, I would say we will linger for a good many more years.

Despite the relative gains that women have made over the last 30 years, in absolute terms there are still significant gaps. For example, in my own profession, while women represent as much as 30% of associates employed by a group of large law firms surveyed by *The National Law Journal* in 1984, only 5% of the partnership positions were occupied by women. In Washington, fewer than 5 out of every 100 members of the 100th Congress are women. Fewer than 5% of the nation's judges are women.

Some of these disparities must be attributed to women's late start in these areas. Yet some also must be attributed to tenacious cultural and social barriers. But I am sure you agree with me that society as a whole benefits immeasurably from a climate in which all persons, regardless of race or gender, may have the opportunity to earn respect, responsibility, advancement, and remuneration based on ability, and from a climate in which those who do achieve success are concerned about those who cannot provide for themselves.

Despite the encouraging and wonderful gains and changes for women that have occurred in my lifetime, there is still room to advance and to promote correction of the remaining deficiencies and imbalances. Let us look forward to completing the task of helping to make real the promise of equal justice under law.

REFERENCES

Anthony, K. 1958. *First Lady of the Revolution*. Garden City, NY: Doubleday & Co., Inc.

Board of Directors of Rotary International v. Rotary Club of Duarte. 1987. 107 S. Ct. 1940.

Bradwell v. Illinois. 1872. 83 U.S. 16 Wall. 130.

Brown v. Board of Education. 1954. 347 U.S. 483.

Craig v. Boren. 1976. 429 U.S. 190.

Frontiero v. Richardson. 1973. 411 U.S. 677.

Goesaert v. Cleary. 1948. 335 U.S. 464.

Green, J. 1982. *Morrow's International Dictionary of Contemporary Quotations*.

Hishon v. King & Spalding. 1984. 467 U.S. 69.

Hoyt v. Florida. 1961. 368 U.S. 57.

Johnson v. Transportation Agency. 1987. 107 S. Ct. 1442.

Kirchberg v. Feenstra. 1981. 450 U.S. 455.

McNamara, M. F. 1967. *2,000 Famous Legal Quotations*.

Meritor Savings Bank, FSB v. Vinson. 1986. 106 S. Ct. 2399.

Minor v. Happersett. 1874. 88 U.S. 21 Wall. 162.

Muller v. Oregon. 1908. 208 U.S. 412.

Norton, Mary Beth. 1980. *Liberty's Daughters: The Revolutionary Experience of American Women, 1750-1800*. Boston: Little, Brown and Company.

Orr v. Orr. 1979. 440 U.S. 268.

Reed v. Reed. 1971. 404 U.S. 71.

Roberts v. Jaycees. 1984. 468 U.S. 609.

Roe v. Wade. 1973. 410 U.S. 113.

Slaughter-House Cases. 1872. 83 U.S. 16 Wall. 36.

Stanton v. Stanton. 1975. 421 U.S. 7.

Strauder v. West Virginia. 1880. 100 U.S. 303.

Taylor v. Louisiana. 1975. 419 U.S. 522.

Weinberger v. Wiesenfeld. 1975. 420 U.S. 636.

The Columbian Patriot: Mercy Otis Warren and the Constitution

Larry M. Lane
Judith J. Lane

SUMMARY. The name of Mercy Otis Warren is generally not included among those of the founders of the American republic. Yet there were few individuals of her day who were more consistently dedicated in both deeds and words to the proposition that the new nation should be founded on true republican principles. She deserves a preeminent position among the active participants in the American Revolution. She was a significant force in the debates leading to the ratification of the Constitution and to the eventual adoption of the Bill of Rights. She was the only contemporary woman to write a comprehensive history of the American Revolution, and she was the only historian of the time to write from a republican viewpoint. She successfully balanced traditional femininity with principled political and intellectual activism. Her contemporary influence makes her truly a participating founder of the nation.

On the principles of republicanism was this constitution founded; on these it must stand.

Historical accounts of the founding years of the American republic have traditionally stressed the contributions of famous men; the few politically active women of the period are only now beginning to receive the attention they deserve. During the late eighteenth century, there were a number of thoughtful, educated, and politically active women who voiced their beliefs with eloquence, courage, and unfailing common sense. One of these rare and too often

Larry M. Lane is affiliated with Virginia Polytechnic Institute and State University. Judith J. Lane is affiliated with Shenandoah College and Conservatory.

neglected stars in America's early political firmament was Mercy Otis Warren, a significant figure in the intellectual life and political affairs of the early years of the nation. Her influence extended far beyond her native Massachusetts—largely as the result of her widely circulated political writings and her personal relationships with many of the prominent political figures of the time. She was a significant participant in both the revolutionary establishment and the constitutional founding of the republic. With singular grace, Warren balanced the conflicting requirements of the socially accepted role of women in her time with the demands of her inquiring intellect and her marked literary and political talent.

THE TRADITIONAL WOMAN AND THE REVOLUTIONARY POLITICIAN

Mercy Warren was a curious amalgam of the traditional and the unorthodox. She had the rare good fortune to be educated at the side of her brothers as they prepared for college under the tutelage of her uncle, Reverend Jonathan Russell. He supplied books and educational guidance that opened to her the world of classical literature, politics, religion, and philosophy that was routinely denied girls of that era. At the same time, although her education was unusual, she self-consciously accepted and appeared genuinely to enjoy the conventional role of woman as homemaker, housekeeper, wife, and mother (Norton 1980, 39).

Warren was the devoted mother of five sons, steadfastly believing that her first responsibility was their nurture and education. She also enjoyed a remarkably loving relationship with her husband, who after many years of marriage still addressed her in correspondence as "my dearest friend" and who, when he was 64, wrote her what could only be described as a love letter calling her "my little angel" (Fritz 1972, 259). Warren was thoroughly feminine, and yet she was called to activities beyond the normal sphere of an eighteenth-century matron. Warren's youth was spent in a politically aware and active family. Her married life had at its core a commitment, deeply shared by both her and her husband, to the politics of Massachusetts and, later, to the newly formed republic of America. As her political circle broadened from immediate family and relatives to include close friends, local political associates, revolutionaries, constitution makers, and leaders of the new republic, her area of influence subtly widened.

During the Revolutionary period, Warren's unusual mix of characteristics went beyond that of what Linda Kerber (1980) has termed "The Republican Mother"—skilled, educated, dedicated to civic virtue and morality, integrating political values into domestic life (11, 229); she was, according to Kerber, "virtually the only prominent American example who could be trotted out against the complaint that intellect necessarily meant rejection of domesticity and of domestic work" (227). Throughout her life, Warren insisted on combining her conventional domestic life with her abiding interest in ideas and events outside her Plymouth, Massachusetts, home. She was both homemaker and political propagandist, mother and revolutionary.

While it was not extraordinary for women in relatively affluent circumstances to engage in educational and literary pursuits, nor was it unheard of for such women to express political opinions, these activities conventionally were confined to the immediate family circle, or at most to personal correspondence and diaries (Kerber 1980, 10-11). Warren's orbit of interest extended well beyond closeted opinion and state politics as she became a respected author of poetry, of politically inflammatory plays, and later of a significant three-volume work of history covering the entire scope of the American Revolution. She was not only exceptional because she was a direct and prominent participant in the swirling tide of events that gave birth to the Revolution; she was unique as a woman writing political propaganda excoriating the British and their colonial loyalists. During the Revolution, she publicly challenged the enemy: "Be it known unto Britain," she wrote, "even American daughters are politicians and patriots, and will aid the good work" (DePauw 1975, 160).

Warren and her husband James, along with John and Abigail Adams, Benjamin Church, Samuel Adams, John Hancock, and her brother James Otis, Jr., formed the nucleus of a group of patriots who kept alive the ideal of liberty in the face of ever-tightening English colonial demands. The Warrens' Plymouth dinner table was the scene of more than one meeting convened to discuss the narrowing alternatives open to colonists as their liberties were increasingly threatened by a myopic mother country. Warren's revolutionary activity, in the forefront of political events, makes fully appropriate the title of "First Lady of the Revolution" bestowed on her by her sympathetic biographer, Katharine Anthony (1958).

The years of the first fledgling steps of the republic and the framing of the Constitution must have been especially poignant for Warren. By 1787 she was an "old revolutionary," a vocal member of the generation of men and women who had fought for the Revolution but who were being eclipsed by younger men who were dissatisfied with the ineffectiveness of the political system established under the Articles of Confederation (Maier 1980). As she argued publicly for liberty and for republican principles, Warren contended in this endeavor with a host of brilliant, articulate, and argumentative men. Again she found herself involved in a role beyond the feminine norm. She became virtually the only woman who was politically active and influential at the national level in the period 1787-1788.

IDEALISM: THE ANTI-FEDERALIST

On August 2, 1787, Warren wrote to her friend Catherine Macaulay, the prominent English historian, about the ongoing Constitutional Convention: "Every man of sense is convinced a strong, efficient Government is necessary; but the old patriots wish to see a form established on the pure principles of Republicanism" (C. Warren 1929, 378). Warren cherished the memory of the Revolution and the struggle against arbitrary authority and distant, monarchical government. She had a "bone deep" dislike of aristocracy, and she shared with other like-minded citizens a profound suspicion of the secrecy surrounding the Constitutional Convention in Philadelphia (Anthony 1958, 155). Warren expressed a theory of republicanism drawn directly from classical political philosophy. Her first principle was that the government was the servant and not the master of the people; as she stated it, "the origin of all power is in the people" (Storing 1981, v. 4, 274). Second, the republic had to be small in order to maintain its community solidarity and commonalty of interest—her model was the city-state of ancient Greece. She believed in the importance of local affiliations within a small territory, accompanied by the requirements of citizenship, civic virtue, and participation in the governing process. In her view, public service in the public interest needed to be governed by "disinterestedness," not by personal ambition (Main 1961b). Within the republic, political morality, virtue, and clearly defined standards of right and justice were essential (Kenyon 1973).

Warren's positive view of what a republic should be was accompanied by a specific, vehemently articulated litany of political evils to be avoided in a republican polity. These included personal ambition and interest, avarice, luxury, aristocracy, nobility, tyranny, and despotism. The potential for political corruption was a primary concern: A major issue, perhaps a principal cause, of the Revolution had been the perception by the colonists of English governmental corruption (Bailyn 1968; Wood 1972). As early as 1773, in her propaganda play, *The Adulateur*, Warren protested against the corruption of office-holding (M. Warren 1980). In 1787, she was still greatly concerned about evidence in America of the private ambition for power and "a rage for the accumulation of wealth by a kind of public gambling instead of private industry" (C. Warren 1929, 379). The sins of personal ambition and private interest seemed to her to be leading to a falling away from the morality that was fundamental to a republic (Smith 1966, 115).

Warren had long been concerned about an appropriate constitution for the new nation that would guard against political corruption. In 1775 she had advised John Adams that a constitution should be created "with such symmetry of Features, such Vigour of Nerves, and such strength of sinew, that it may never be in the power of Ambition or Tyranny to shake the durable Fabrick" (Fritz 1972, 150). In 1787 she felt even more cause for concern. In Philadelphia, what Fred Barbash (1987) has called "one of the greatest all-male clubs in history" was debating and constructing a new constitution for the nation (A9). Symmetry and vigor and sinew were being created, but the document that emerged from the Convention caused Warren and others grave concern about its fostering of ambition and its "awful squintings"—as Patrick Henry phrased it—towards monarchy (Elliot 1901, v. 3, 43-64).

In Warren's view, the inescapable problem with the proposed

Constitution was that it failed to meet the standard of pure republican principles. Warren was concerned that the document was not the product of the Revolutionary generation but of younger men who saw opportunities for advancement and power (Maier 1980). She was further disturbed when her good friend and confidant, Elbridge Gerry, declined to add his signature to the final product (Fritz 1972, 244). For Warren, this Constitution, with its accompanying arguments for energy of government and a strengthened executive, clearly opened the door to arbitrary central authority, aristocracy, and corruption.

Even more disturbing to Warren was the failure of the proposed Constitution to protect individuals through some version of a bill of rights. The fearful prospect of a lost republic motivated Warren to join with her husband in forming the nucleus of an embryonic political party that came to be identified with the Anti-Federalists (Main 1961b, 119). In 1787, at age 60, Warren reentered the political wars in opposition to the aggressive and ambitious men who were responsible for "the fraudulent usurpation at Philadelphia" and who were distorting and endangering her image of the republic that she believed America should be (Storing 1981, v. 4, 283).

In the rapid pace of the ratification process, the Anti-Federalist opposition to the Constitution in Massachusetts was unable to block ratification; however, an example of recommended amendments was established in the Massachusetts convention, which substantially influenced ratification actions in other states. Once again, Warren's political activity and influence transcended her local base. Under a pen name ("A Columbian Patriot"), she authored a pamphlet that effectively summarized the Anti-Federalist position. Her comprehensive argument (18 indictments in three categories) against the proposed Constitution (Smith 1966, 109; Storing 1981, v. 4, 270-287) was published in time to be utilized widely in the ratification debates in New York, where more than 1600 copies were distributed—a circulation that exceeded that of the *Federalist* essays of Hamilton, Madison, and Jay (DePauw 1966, 113).

Nationally, although the Anti-Federalists lost the ratification battle, their arguments and reasoning provided an essential foundation for the new republic in their concepts of republicanism, citizenship, public virtue, and morality (Rohr 1986, 10). In expressing these fundamental arguments, Mercy Warren was articulate, representative, and influential. As the Columbian Patriot, she is cited by James McGregor Burns (1982, 58ff) as the spokesperson for the entire Anti-Federalist argument. For Burns this is a qualified compliment, since he uses Warren's essay to illustrate the lesser sophistication of the Anti-Federalist position as compared with the more persuasive arguments of the Federalists. Still, it may be fairly said that the Anti-Federalists' arguments, and Warren's idealism, were necessary—even if not alone sufficient—for the future governance of the American nation. The successful republic was the product of an essential mix of the ideals of republicanism and the realities of political action to establish and govern the country.

REALISM: THE CONSTITUTIONAL REPUBLICAN

During the summer of the Philadelphia Convention, Warren expressed a certain resignation about the outcome when she wrote to Elbridge Gerry, the one delegate she fully trusted, "Yet some of us have lived long enough not to expect everything great, good, and excellent from so imperfect a creature as man . . . therefore [I] shall not be disappointed either at the mouse or the mountain that this long labor may produce" (Fritz 1972, 244). Still, Warren believed that this Constitution was too important to leave either to chance or to the invention of others. At about the same time that she was writing to Gerry, she was also expressing her concern and her hope to Catherine Macaulay:

> God grant that a system may be devised that will give energy to law and dignity to Government, without demolishing the work of their own hands, without leveling the fair fabric of a free, strong and National Republic, beneath the splendid roof of royal or aristocratic pageantry. (C. Warren 1929, 379)

Following ratification, Warren became a willing participant in the remarkable closing of ranks of all parties behind the idea and reality of the Constitution and the government that was formed under its provisions (Wren 1985, 389-408). In this, Warren was a political realist. She did not abandon her republican ideals. Instead, she continually held reality to the standard of those ideals. When reality fell short or moved away from her vision of republicanism, as it did in her assessment of the actions of Washington, Hamilton, and Adams, she addressed the issues and sought remedies. By the mid-1790s, the Warrens of Massachusetts had become staunch supporters of the party of Jefferson and Madison, participating fully in the development of a new dynamic in the politics of the nation.

In Warren's support for the newly ratified Constitution, she demonstrated her "old Otis respect for political realities" (Fritz 1972, 255). She and most of the Anti-Federalists were appeased by the quick passage of the Bill of Rights, which they believed came as a direct result of their activities during the ratification campaigns. On April 2, 1789, Warren advised John Adams that she was persuaded "that the new government will operate very quietly unless the reins are held too taut" (Fritz 1972, 254). Over time, she found it possible to go even further than acceptance: "Mrs. Warren not only accepted the Constitution after amendment, but no Federalist exceeded her extravagant praise" (Smith 1966, 109). Eventually, she was able to write in her *History of the Rise, Progress and Termination of the American Revolution*, "But the system was adopted with expectations of amendment, and the experiment proved salutary, and has ultimately redounded as much to the honor and interest of America, as any mode or form of government that could have been devised by the wisdom of man" (M. Warren 1970, v. 3, 368-369).

Such a salutary outcome had not been assured from the beginning. In Warren's view, the 12 ascendant years of the Federalists (1789-1800), with their monarchical and aristocratic tendencies, were an aberration and not an indictment of the Constitution. She made this point forcefully in one of her later letters to John Adams: "The principles of that Constitution have been admired, but the deviations from them detested, and the corrupt practices and arbitrary systems of that Government are become abhorrent" (Adams 1972, 331). Warren believed that the Federalists in general and John Adams in particular had attempted to hold the reins "too taut" and had "relinquished the republican system, and forgotten the principles of the American revolution" (M. Warren 1970, v. 3, 392).

For Warren, the true spirit of the Constitution was adequate to its worldwide significance and to the principles of republicanism. In fairness to the Federalists, they had successfully created and established a governmental system that had fostered effective governance and that also provided a framework within which republicanism ultimately could prevail (Kenyon 1973, 85). Thus the Constitutional system provided a foundation for democracy, which was realized by the victory in 1800 of Jefferson and his party. A Federalist framework with a republican spirit and leadership became the formula for the achievement of the political and economic requirements of the young republic. For Warren, political union and a vigorous economy were important (Anthony 1958, 169-170; Smith 1966, 106-107). To have them in a republican context was essential.

In 1805, Warren completed the documentation of her beliefs and her firsthand knowledge of the events of the latter half of the eighteenth century with the publication of her remarkable *History of the Rise, Progress and Termination of the American Revolution*, the first two and one-half volumes of which were devoted specifically to the events prior to and contemporary with the Revolution. This was a thoroughly documented, well researched, and effectively written chronicle, completed over a period of 20 years, which drew heavily on her firsthand acquaintance with many participants as well as on previously published sources. The last half of her third volume covered events from the end of the war until 1801 and was completed by Warren at age 77. The work has been characterized by one historian as "a vast morality play—strikingly similar to the plays she wrote in the 1770s" (Cohen 1980, 203, 210).

Warren's *History* aroused the now famous ire of John Adams. Adams felt that his contributions had been neglected by his longtime friend and, worse, that she had sullied and blackened his reputation. The publication of the *History* precipitated an extraordinary exchange of correspondence between Adams and Warren in which the two former friends and political allies freely assaulted each other's good name and reputation (Adams 1972). Adams' reaction to the *History* was predictable. Ever sensitive and insecure, he was convinced of the propriety of his political decisions but was apprehensive about the final verdict history would make concerning his administration.

In the *History*, Warren was unable to disguise her political biases as she took Adams to task for his apparent preference for things monarchical after his ministerial assignments abroad, and for his support of the Alien and Sedition Acts. Their exchange of letters concerning her printed remarks is revealing—both of the intensity of their individual political beliefs and of the extraordinary sensitivity of each to the opinion of the other. Warren's strength of character was fully revealed when she finally and defiantly said to Adams, "Though I am fatigued with your repetition of abuse, I am not intimidated" (Adams 1972, 454).

Warren's *History* was the only history of the times that was written by a contemporary woman. It was also the only contemporary treatment of the period written from a republican point of view (Fritz 1972, 294). Aside from Warren, the historical record of the period was produced by Federalists. Thus, as William Raymond Smith (1966, 101) points out, the last half of Volume 3 reads like a minority report on the founding of the republic. She wrote her history, as Bernard Bailyn (1967) states it, "entirely in the spirit of the Revolutionary pamphleteers" (64). This assessment demonstrates Warren's lifelong political consistency: In her 40s and 50s she was a revolutionary agitator; in her 60s she was an Anti-Federalist activist as well as a poet and playwright; and in her 70s she was a republican historian. Her *History* serves to underscore that always, until the end of her life, she was first and foremost a devoted republican, faithful to her principles and to her sense of morality and the dignity and rights of man.

THE CONSTITUTIONAL SYNTHESIS OF MERCY OTIS WARREN

Following his election to the Presidency, Thomas Jefferson wrote compassionate and encouraging words to James Warren:

> I have seen with great grief yourself and so many venerable patriots retired and weeping in silence over the subversion of those principles for the attainment of which you had sacrificed the ease and comforts of life; . . . I pray you to present my homage of my great respect to Mrs. Warren. I have long pos-

> sessed evidence of her high station in the ranks of genius and have considered her silence a proof that she did not go with the current. (Anthony 1958, 198)

Mercy Warren responded to Jefferson herself: "It is true, Sir, that she has not gone with the current. None of her family has ever gone with the current, though borne down by a strong tide for want of suppleness to the system of the late Administration; with becoming firmness they have met its frowns, nor have ever wavered in the storm" (Anthony 1958, 198). Indeed, Warren spent her entire life going against the current. She consistently overcame the obstacles of her gender, her times, and her own occasional sense of inadequacy and inappropriateness. In 1814, in the final year of her life, she was still standing on principle as she actively supported Mr. Madison's war against the British, speaking out against the popular sentiment in Massachusetts and against her own family's financial interest.

For Warren, not going with the current meant that, although her political principles had to live in the real world, they must never be sacrificed to political expediency. In this, she personified the unique and extraordinarily difficult requirements of the American political experiment. The constitutional system requires active politics and the contention of interests and ambition; however, it also requires the disinterestedness of public service and the ideals of civic virtue and community interest. The Constitution requires checks and balances not just among institutions but also among the conflicting imperatives of morality and power. This is difficult in any polity, or in any personality, but Warren consciously attempted to find that balance. The difficulty of the task can be found in her own words (Main 1961a, 186):

> Our situation is truly delicate and critical. On the one hand, we stand in need of a strong federal government, founded on principles that will support the prosperity and union of the Colonies. On the other, we have struggled for liberty and made costly sacrifices at her shrine and there are still many among us who revere her name too much to relinquish, beyond a certain medium, the rights of man for the dignity of government.

The turn of the century brought political vindication for Warren. In a broad sense, the election of Jefferson completed the American constitutional symmetry. The triumph of the Democratic Republicans represented the political merger of energy and liberty, of power and democratic morality. The genius of Warren was to align herself actively with this synthesis and to represent it in her life. In this she had the better of her argument with John Adams, who, as Gordon Wood (1972) notes, was "isolated from the main line of American intellectual development" (569). She had the better of her disagreement with Hamilton, who was at once "premature and out of date" in his desire to model the government after the British "court" system of the eighteenth century (Banning 1984, 27-28). Clearly, the near future of the American experiment belonged to Warren's republican principles and to the political philosophy of Jefferson and Madison.

The long-term future of the American republic was another question. In addition to her other qualities, Warren was something of a pessimist about the capacity of the American people to continue in liberty, freedom, and republicanism. In an early poem written in 1778, she had asked:

> Shall freedom's cause by vice be thus betray'd?—
> Behold the schedule that unfolds the crimes
> and marks the manners of these modern times.
>
> —M. Warren 1980, 246

Years later, she characterized the American people as "too proud for monarchy, yet too poor for nobility, and it is to be feared, too selfish and avaricious for a virtuous republic" (1970, v. 3, 370). She was continually distressed by what she perceived to be the weakness of the American moral fabric and the selfish spirit of the times. In this she stood with Jefferson, who in his first inaugural address called on the American people to guard "against a rising tide of individualism and acquisitiveness" (Morris 1987, 29).

Warren has been likened to an Old Testament prophet crying out "against the sins of her generation" (Smith 1966, 110). However, her Puritanism was subdued and secondary. She never called for a return to an idealized golden age of virtue. She consistently demonstrated a greater concern for the present and the future than for the past (Cohen 1980, 200), and in fact she saw the future with remarkable prescience. Two months before her death at age 86, she wrote her last letter to John Adams: "Will things remain thus? I say, No. There are seeds of other revolutions which, in a few short years or months, may pour out torrents of blood and misery on a guilty world" (Adams 1972, 510). Thus her consistent exhortation to the American people was the necessity of upholding republican principles and living in righteousness and virtue. In this she spoke the languages of her Puritan religion and of her unwavering republicanism—languages that are fundamental to the American political experience (see Bellah et al. 1985).

Warren survived the political struggles of Revolution, Constitution, and the early years of the republic with her integrity and her faith intact. She hoped that the daring experiment of a nation founded on strictly republican principles, peopled by a virtuous citizenry, could and would work, and it was to that end that she devoted her political life and talent, first as a revolutionary republican, later as a constitutional realist, and finally and always as an advocate for what she believed to be truth and civic virtue. As a writer and a political thinker, Warren was an unswerving force for vital qualities in the context of the American constitutional system—unquestionably a founder and heroine of the republic.

REFERENCES

Adams, Charles F., ed. 1972. *Correspondence Between John Adams and Mercy Warren*. New York: Arno Press. (Reprinted from Collections of the Massachusetts Historical Society, v. 4, 5th series, Boston, 1878.)

Anthony, Katharine. 1958. *First Lady of the Revolution: The Life of Mercy Otis Warren*. Garden City, NY: Doubleday & Company, Inc.

Bailyn, Bernard. 1967. *The Ideological Origins of the American Revolution*. Cambridge, MA: The Belknap Press.

Bailyn, Bernard. 1968. *The Origins of American Politics*. New York: Vintage Books.

Banning, Lance. January 1984. The Hamiltonian Madison: A Reconsideration. *The Virginia Magazine of History and Biography*, 92:3-28.

Barbash, Fred. "The Founders: An All Male Club." *The Washington Post*, 13 July 1987.

Bellah, Robert N., Richard Madsen, William M. Sullivan, Ann Swidler, and

Steven M. Tipton. 1985. *Habits of the Heart: Individualism and Commitment in American Life*. Berkeley, CA: University of California Press.

Burns, James MacGregor. 1982. *The Vineyard of Liberty: The American Experiment*. New York: Alfred A. Knopf.

Cohen, L. H. 1980. "Explaining the Revolution: Ideology and Ethics in Mercy Otis Warren's Historical Theory." *The William and Mary Quarterly*, 3rd series, 37:200-218.

DePauw, Linda Grant. 1966. *The Eleventh Pillar: New York State and the Federal Constitution*. Ithaca, NY: Cornell University Press.

DePauw, Linda Grant. 1975. *Founding Mothers: Women in America in the Revolutionary Era*. Boston: Houghton Mifflin Company.

Elliot, Jonathan, ed. 1901. *The Debates in the Several State Conventions, on the Adoption of the Federal Constitution*, 3rd ed. Philadelphia: J. B. Lippincott Company.

Fritz, Jean. 1972. *Cast for a Revolution: Some American Friends and Enemies, 1728-1814*. Boston: Houghton Mifflin Company.

Kenyon, Cecelia M. 1973. "Men of Little Faith: The Anti-Federalists on the Nature of Representative Government." In *The Confederation and the Constitution: The Critical Issues*, ed. Gordon S. Wood. Boston: Little, Brown and Company.

Kerber, Linda K. 1980. *Women of the Republic: Intellect and Ideology in Revolutionary America*. Chapel Hill, NC: The University of North Carolina Press.

Maier, Pauline. 1980. *The Old Revolutionaries: Political Lives in the Age of Samuel Adams*. New York: Alfred A. Knopf.

Main, Jackson Turner. 1961a. *The Antifederalists: Critics of the Constitution, 1781-1788*. Chapel Hill, NC: The University of North Carolina Press.

Main, Jackson Turner. 1961b. *Political Parties Before the Constitution*. Chapel Hill, NC: The University of North Carolina Press.

Morris, Richard B. 1987. *The Forging of the Union: 1781-1789*. New York: Harper & Row, Publishers.

Norton, Mary Beth. 1980. *Liberty's Daughters: The Revolutionary Experience of American Women, 1750-1800*. Boston: Little, Brown and Company.

Rohr, John A. 1986. *To Run a Constitution: The Legitimacy of the Administrative State*. Lawrence, KS: University Press of Kansas.

Smith, William Raymond. 1966. *History as Argument: Three Patriot Historians of the American Revolution*. The Hague: Mouton & Co.

Storing, Herbert J. 1981. *The Complete Anti-Federalist*, 6 vols. Chicago: The University of Chicago Press.

Warren, Charles. 1929. *The Making of the Constitution*. Boston: Little, Brown, and Company.

Warren, Mercy. 1970. *History of the Rise, Progress and Termination of the American Revolution: Interspersed With Biographical, Political and Moral Observations*, 3 vols. New York: AMS Press. (Reprinted from the Boston edition of 1805.)

Warren, Mercy Otis. 1980. *The Plays and Poems of Mercy Otis Warren: Facsimile*

Reproductions. Compiled and with an introduction by Benjamin Franklin V. Delmar, NY: Scholars' Facsimiles and Reprints.

Wood, Gordon S. 1972. *The Creation of the American Republic, 1776-1787*. New York: W. W. Norton & Company.

Wren, J. Thomas. October 1985. The Ideology of Court and Country in the Virginia Ratifying Convention of 1788. *The Virginia Magazine of History and Biography*, 93:389-408.

From Three-Fifths to Zero: Implications of the Constitution for African-American Women, 1787-1870

Mamie E. Locke

SUMMARY. In 1987 the United States began celebrations marking the bicentennial of the Constitution. As these celebrations occur, it is important to discuss some of the implications of that document for African-American women. This paper examines the struggle for "wholeness" of the African-American woman, who evolved initially as three-fifths of a person in 1787 and moved to zero with the passage of the Fifteenth Amendment in 1870. Despite their hard-fought, sometimes subtle, battles against racism and sexism, the Fifteenth Amendment underscored their omission and their marginal status under the supreme law of the land – the Constitution.

During the summer months of 1787, in Philadelphia, Pennsylvania, 55 men argued, debated, suggested, compromised, and eventually hammered out a document that would form the basis of the government of the United States of America. In 1788, the requisite number of states had ratified this document – the Constitution. The Constitution has been called a living, flexible piece of work that is the cornerstone of American democracy. It has been argued that the Constitution established the privileges and rights of citizenship, raised to new heights the rights of individuals, and acknowledged the fundamental principles of life, liberty, and the pursuit of happiness. In the bicentennial year of the ratification of the United States Constitution, a simple question can be posed: Was the primacy of individual rights and equality truly reflected in the Constitution as it was written in 1787? The response to this question is equally sim-

---

Mamie E. Locke is affiliated with Hampton University.

ple: no, given the omission, for various reasons, of more than half the population. At the bottom of the heap of omissions was to be found the African-American woman.

In his controversial remarks on the bicentennial of the Constitution, U.S. Supreme Court Justice Thurgood Marshall argued that the meaning of the Constitution was not "fixed" in 1787; furthermore, the wisdom, sense of justice, and foresight of the framers who are being hailed in celebration was not all that profound, particularly since they created a defective government from the beginning. Marshall further stated that there were intentional omissions, namely blacks and women (Marshall 1987, 2). It is the purpose of this paper to discuss a group of people encompassing both characteristics of exclusion—African-American women. It is also the purpose of this paper to elaborate on Justice Marshall's interpretation of the meaning of the Constitution, specifically as it relates to the document's exclusion of African-American women in 1787 and again in 1870. Also to be discussed are African-American women's struggles against peripheral status and the consequences of exclusion.

The framers of the Constitution were careful to avoid using terms designating sex or color. The words "slave," "slavery," and "female" are not to be found in the original document. What one does find are phrases such as "persons held to service or labor" (Article IV, section 2) or "three fifths of all other persons" (Article I, section 2). Those persons held to service or labor and designated as three fifths were African-Americans, females and males. Thus the African-American woman started her life in this new government created by men of "wisdom, foresight and a sense of justice," as three-fifths of a person. The struggle for wholeness was begun almost immediately, yet the African-American woman usually found herself on the periphery of such struggles. She participated, but she watched as her status moved from three-fifths, in the 1787 document, to zero—total exclusion—with the passage of the Fifteenth Amendment in 1870.

Once, when a speaker at an antislavery meeting praised the Constitution, Sojourner Truth, that prolific sage of the nineteenth century, responded in this way:

> Children, I talks to God and God talks to me. I go out and talks to God in de fields and de woods. Dis morning I was walking out and I got over de fence. I saw de wheat a holding up its head, looking very big. I goes up and talks holt of it. You b'lieve it, dere was no wheat dere. I says, 'God, what is de matter wid dis wheat?' and he says to me, 'Sojourner, dere is a little weasel in it.' Now I hears talkin' bout de Constitution and de rights of man. I come up and talks holt of dis Constitution. It looks mighty big, and I feels for my rights, but dere ain't any dere. Den I say, 'God, what ails dis Constitution?' He says to me, 'Sojourner, dere is a little weasel in it.' (Bennett 1964, 146)

Thus, when the Constitution was written, it advocated equality, opportunity, and the rights of all, yet it condoned the institution of slavery, where men and women alike were reduced to property. Or were they persons? In the Federalist #54, James Madison argued that slaves were considered not only as property but also as persons under the federal Constitution. According to Madison, "the true state of the case is that they partake of both these qualities; being considered by our laws, in some respects, as persons, and in other respects, as property . . . the Federal Constitution . . . views them [slaves] in the mixt character" (Madison 1961, 337). In this essay, Madison sought to explain the use of such "weasel" phraseology as "three fifths of all other persons" and "the migration or importation of such persons" (Article I, section 9).

When antislavery advocates compromised their principles and allowed the institution of slavery to be sanctioned by the very foundation of the new government, the Constitution, they relegated the African-American to a status of insignificance. The three-fifths compromise, by counting African-Americans for the purpose of taxation and representation, created an interesting paradox. It gave to African-Americans the dual status of person and property—however, more property than person.

What did all this mean for the African-American woman? Involuntary servitude had a tremendous impact on African-Americans, as it was both an economic and a political institution designed to manipulate and exploit men and women. As active participants in the labor market during the slavery era, African-American women worked not only in the plantation fields and in the masters' homes but in their own homes as well. They took on many roles and virtually had to be everything to everybody. They were, inter alia, mothers, lovers (willing and unwilling), laborers, and producers of labor. After 1808, the supply of slaves abated somewhat due to congressional legislation prohibiting the importation of Africans into the country. Consequently, the source of additional slave labor was to be effected through natural increase. Once again the onus was on the shoulders of the African-American woman, who fell prey to further victimization and exploitation. Her fertility was viewed as an asset, yet she had no control over the children born to her; they, too, were the property of the slave owner, to be bought and sold at the owner's demand.

Interpretation of the Constitution and state laws and statutes merely reinforced the notion of the property rights of slaveholders. For example, the defeminization of African-American women made it easy for them to be exploited: They "were never too pregnant, too young, too frail, to be subject to the harsh demands of an insensitive owner" (Horton 1986, 53). African-American women were not allowed the protections that were accorded to white women. They were expected to work hard for the slave owner and to maintain their own homes as well. Their status can be summed up in the folk wisdom given to Janie Sparks by her grandmother in Zora Neale Hurston's novel, *Their Eyes Were Watching God*:

> De white man throw down the load and tell de nigger man to pick it up. He pick it up because he have to, but he don't tote it. He hand it to his womenfolks. De nigger woman is de mule of the world so far as Ah can see. (Hurston 1969, 29)

The seeds of this reality for the African-American woman were planted in slavery. Hence, African-American women had few illusions that they held the favored position accorded white women.

African-American women did not complacently accept their lot in life. They engaged in resistance in many ways (see Davis 1971, and Hine and Wittenstein 1981). They also initiated their own groups such as literary societies and temperance, charitable, and education groups, and of course antislavery groups. Although some white feminists of the nineteenth century, such as Lucy Stone and Susan B. Anthony, invited African-American women to participate in the women's struggle, the reform groups actively discriminated against African-American women. Their dislike of slavery did not extend to an acceptance of African-Americans as equals. For example, attempts by African-American women to participate in a meeting of an antislavery society in Massachusetts nearly caused the collapse of that group. According to historical documents, African-American men were more readily accepted into the inner sanctums of abolitionist societies than were African-American women. It is no surprise, then, that the most well-known advocates of women's rights among African-Americans were males, e.g., Frederick Douglass, James Forte (Sr. and Jr.), and Robert Purvis. The most prominent female was Sojourner Truth (Terborg-Penn 1981, 303). African-American women did, however, participate through their own initiative in both the antislavery and women's movements.

Armed with beliefs such as "It is not the color of the skin that makes the man or woman, but the principle formed in the soul" (Stewart 1973, 565), women such as the Forten sisters, Maria Stewart, and Milla Granson, to name a few, spoke out against racial and sexual injustices. For example, Maria Stewart often attacked racial injustice in the United States. Her outspokenness was accepted and applauded by African-American men until her criticisms were aimed at them for not doing as much as they could for the race. Stewart realized then the limitations placed on her as an African-American woman. She could speak out on behalf of civil rights and abolition but could not address sexism among African-American men. This dilemma, or duality of oppression, is a burden that African-American women still bear.

In the period preceding the Civil War, African-American and white men and women worked together as abolitionists. All saw a future where slaves and women would be liberated and elevated to equal status under the Constitution of the United States. But would this Constitution incorporate women and slaves? Political abolitionists and Garrisonian abolitionists (followers of William Lloyd Garrison) debated the role and the significance of the Constitution. Many felt that the American political system was corrupt and that this corruption stemmed from the Constitution. As a Garrisonian, Frederick Douglass felt that supporting the Constitution was also supporting slavery. He argued that endorsement of the Constitution meant that one served two masters, liberty and slavery. This argument was articulated also by abolitionist Wendell Phillips. Phillips felt that one should not hold an office in which an oath of allegiance to the Constitution was required. He argued that, since the Constitution was a document upholding slavery, anyone who supported it was a participant in the moral guilt of the institution of slavery (Hofstadter 1948, 148; Lobel 1987, 20).

Douglass later moved away from the Garrisonian view and came to support the political abolitionists' natural-law theory. This view of the Constitution justified participation in the political process (Garrisonians argued for nonparticipation in government), which would allow radical lawyers and judges to argue against and eventually end slavery. It is the natural-law interpretation of the Constitution that led Douglass to assert that the three-fifths compromise "leans to freedom" (Lobel 1987, 20). But did it in fact? According to Chief Justice Roger Taney in the case of *Dred Scott v. Sandford* (1857), persons of African descent were not citizens under the Constitution. Taney reemphasized the Declaration of Independence's and Constitution's denial of African-American citizenship, for the Constitution, he argued, clearly showed that Africans were not to be regarded as people or citizens under the government formed in 1787; they were, and would continue to be, property.

Even before the *Dred Scott* decision, a future president was voicing his opposition to suffrage and equality for African-Americans: In a letter to the *New Salem Journal* in 1836, Abraham Lincoln wrote that he supported suffrage for all whites, male and female, if they paid taxes or served in the military. In 1858, a year after the infamous *Dred Scott* decision, Lincoln confirmed this view by stating that he in no way advocated social and political equality between whites and blacks and that he was as much in favor as anyone of whites having a superior position over blacks (Catt and Shuler 1969, 70; Hofstadter 1948, 116).

Armed with political agitation, men and women, whites and African-Americans, toiled long and hard toward the quest for equality and liberation. This agitation culminated in a bloody Civil War that ended with the South in ruins and another struggle in store. Who would secure political rights in the postwar period—white women, African-Americans, or both? Where would the African-American woman be, once the smoke cleared?

The democratization of America, it has been said, has not been the result of the Constitution, or of the equalitarian ideals of voters, or even of the demands of nonvoters; however, these things have played a role, albeit a secondary one. What, then, has brought about democratic change in American society? To some observers, the motivating force behind the major democratic reforms has been partisan advantage. Those reforms thought to be advantageous to a political party have passed; others have been shelved (Elliott 1974, 34).

An all-important question during the period following the Civil War was "What is to be done with the freedman?" Senator Charles Summer of Massachusetts felt that African-Americans should be given the ballot and should be treated like men. Thaddeus Stevens of Pennsylvania said they should be given 40 acres of land and should be regarded as human beings. Abraham Lincoln suggested deportation but was told that that idea was virtually impossible (Bennett 1964, 186-187). So what was to be done?

Two groups saw advantages to using the freedmen for their own purposes. First, leaders of the women's rights movement saw an opportunity to channel constitutional discussions around universal suffrage. They supported passage of the Thirteenth Amendment (which ended slavery) and continually pointed out that universal suffrage was a direct outgrowth of the principle of unconditional emancipation. The doors that had formerly been closed to African-Americans were slowly opening. As both federal and state constitutions were amended to accommodate the African-American, women pushed forward, hoping that they could pass through the same doors as the freedmen (DuBois 1987, 845; Papachristou 1976, 48). Women were not to be as lucky as the freedmen, however. With the doors closing to them, conflict was brewing that would lead to an irreparable schism between women and African-Americans, a schism that would carry over to the twentieth century struggles of blacks and women.

The second group looking for personal gain on the backs of the freedmen was the Republican Party. Republican leaders saw an opportunity to consolidate their power base by enfranchising the freedmen. It was felt that African-Americans, out of gratitude, would support the party with their votes. So the wheels were put into motion to enfranchise the freedmen. Were women to be included? Would suffrage be universal?

In 1863, Angelina Grimke stated that the civil and political rights of women and of African-Americans were closely connected. She declared that she wanted to be identified with African-Americans, because women would not get their rights until African-Americans received theirs (Weld 1970, 80). Did this include African-American women, or just men and white women?

President Andrew Johnson opposed granting suffrage to any African-American, male or female. In a meeting with George Downing and Frederick Douglass in 1866, Johnson made his position clear:

> While I say that I am a friend of the colored man, I do not want to adopt a policy that I believe will end in a contest between the races, which if persisted in will result in the extermination of one or the other. . . . Yes, I would be willing to pass with him through the Red sea to the Land of Promise, to the land of liberty; but I am not willing . . . to adopt a policy which I believe will only result in the sacrifice of his life and the shedding of his blood. (Fishel and Quarles 1970, 276)

Despite Johnson's position, the radical Republicans circumvented any of his actions, to the point of impeaching him and nearly convicting him and ousting him from office.

There were national and state fights brewing over the issue of universal suffrage. At the state level, several states, including Kansas and New York, proposed changes to their constitutions advocating suffrage for African-Americans and women. In Kansas both proposals were rejected, whereas in New York the proposal for women was rejected. At the national level, after the Thirteenth Amendment ended slavery, the Fourteenth Amendment was proposed. This amendment created a serious controversy between women suffragists and men. The major area of contention was the wording of the Fourteenth Amendment, which granted suffrage specifically to males. For the first time, the Constitution explicitly defined voters as men. Section 2 reads,

> Representatives shall be apportioned among the several states according to their respective numbers, counting the whole number of persons in each state. . . . But when the right to vote at any election . . . is denied to any of the male inhabitants of such state, being twenty-one years of age, and citizens of the United States . . . the basis of representation therein shall be reduced in the proportion which the number of such male citizens shall bear to the whole number of male citizens twenty-one years of age in such state.

Speaking before the annual meeting of the Equal Rights Association in 1866, Frederick Douglass argued that acquisition of the franchise was vital for African-American men, whereas it was merely desirable for women (Terborg-Penn 1981, 305). Although Douglass attempted to keep the support of white women behind the movement for African-American suffrage, the rift between the two groups was widening.

The greatest controversy arose over the proposal and passage of the Fifteenth Amendment. White women continued to press for universal suffrage but were being told to wait until the suffrage amendment for African-American males had been passed. This time period was deemed the "Negro's hour" (Stanton 1970). The controversy over the Fifteenth Amendment polarized the Equal Rights Association. The Fifteenth Amendment aided the freedmen and rejected women. Where did this leave African-American women? They remained on the periphery as discussion centered on African-American men and white women.

The Equal Rights Association drifted into two factions, the old abolitionists (headed by William Lloyd Garrison, Wendell Phillips, and Frederick Douglass) and the ardent suffragists (headed by Susan B. Anthony and Elizabeth Cady Stanton). The former group argued for support of the Fifteenth Amendment and urged women not to jeopardize the freedmen's opportunity to obtain suffrage. The latter group opposed the Fifteenth Amendment and started its own newspaper, *The Revolution*. This suffragist faction also joined forces with George Train, a racist Democrat (Papachristou 1976, 56); the association with Train exacerbated the already growing rift between the two groups.

The suffragists used *The Revolution* and other forums to voice their opposition to passage of the Fifteenth Amendment. This excerpt from *The Revolution* summarizes their point of view and also includes their views on the position of African-American women:

> Manhood suffrage? Oh! no, my friend, you mistake us, we have enough of that already. We say not another man, black or white, until woman is inside the citadel. What reason have we to suppose the African would be more just and generous than the Saxon has been? Wendell Phillips pleads for black men; we for black women, who have known a degradation and sorrow of slavery such as man has never experienced. (Papachristou 1976, 57)

The issue of African-American women was discussed further in an exchange between Douglass, Anthony, Stanton, and others at a meeting of the Equal Rights Association where the subject of debate was the Fifteenth Amendment. Douglass argued that there was not the same sense of urgency for women as for the freedmen. He indicated that women were not treated as animals, were not insulated or hanged from lampposts, and did not have their children taken from them simply because they were women. When asked if the same things did not happen to African-American women, Douglass replied that they did—but because they were black, not because they were women. Thus Douglass underscored the primacy of race over sex. Elizabeth Stanton argued that if African-American women in the South were not given their rights then their emancipation could be regarded simply as another form of slavery (Papachristou 1976, 64; Stanton 1970, 81). Even though African-American women were victims of both racism and sexism, they were being put in a position of having to choose which oppression was the more debilitating.

Responding to Douglass's remarks, Phoebe Couzins stated, "While feeling extremely willing that the black man shall have all the rights to which he is justly entitled, I consider the claims of the black woman of paramount importance . . . the black women are, and always have been, in a far worse condition than the men. As a class, they are better, and more intelligent than the men, yet they have been subjected to greater brutalities, while compelled to perform exactly the same labor as men toiling by their side in the fields, just as hard burdens imposed upon them, just as severe punishments decreed to them, with the added cares of maternity and household work, with their children taken from them and sold into bondage; suffering a thousandfold more than any man could suffer" (Papachristou 1976, 64). Couzins was one of the few white women who identified with the plight of African-American women and spoke on their behalf. Along with other suffragists, she advocated universal suffrage and felt that the Fifteenth Amendment should not be passed unless women were included. She felt that men were not any more intelligent nor any more deserving than women:

> The Fifteenth Amendment virtually says that every intelligent, virtuous woman is the inferior of every ignorant man, no matter how low he may be sunk into the scale of morality, and every instinct of my being rises to refute such doctrine. (Papachristou 1976, 64)

African-American women were themselves divided over the issue of suffrage. Sojourner Truth spoke for those doubly oppressed by race and sex:

> There is a great stir about colored men getting their rights, but not a word about the colored women; and if colored men get their rights, and not colored women theirs, you see the colored men will be masters over the women, and it will be just as bad as it was before. So I am for keeping the thing going while things are stirring; because if we wait till it is still, it will take a great while to get it going again. (Truth 1973, 569)

Truth supported the Fifteenth Amendment but voiced her concern about men being granted suffrage over women.

The suffragist Frances Harper posed the question whether white women were willing to encompass African-American women in their struggle, to which Anthony and others replied that they were. Harper supported passage of the Fifteenth Amendment; she declared that, if the country could only address one issue at a time, she would rather see African-American men obtain the vote (Papachristou 1976, 64). The debate raged, but when the smoke cleared African-American men had obtained the vote and all women were disenfranchised and remained effectively outside the foundation of the American political system.

It has been argued that the Reconstruction Era focused more attention on the rights of African-Americans and women than ever before (see DuBois 1987, 846). However, it is apparent that the focus was more on the rights of African-American men and white women. African-American women were pushed to the periphery of any discussions, or were acknowledged only nominally, despite the fact that they existed as persons who were both female and black. According to Bell Hooks (1981), the support of African-American male suffrage revealed the depth of sexism, particularly among white males, in American society. To counter this sexism, white women began to urge racial solidarity in opposition to black male suffrage. This placed African-American women in the predicament of choosing between discriminatory precepts—white female racism or African-American patriarchy (Hooks 1981, 3). As Sojourner Truth knew, sexism was as real a threat as racism. This issue remains unsolved.

Because they were excluded from the constitutional furor of the Reconstruction period, especially the controversy surrounding the Fourteenth and Fifteenth Amendments, white female suffragists amplified racist themes in their struggles. They claimed that enfranchising black men created "an aristocracy of sex" because it elevated all men over all women. Women suffragists criticized the Fifteenth Amendment because "a man's government is worse than a white man's government" and because the amendment elevated the "lowest orders of manhood" over "the higher classes of women" (DuBois 1987, 850). They, of course, meant white women.

Passage of the Fifteenth Amendment did not grant universal suffrage, just as the framers were not the proclaimed visionaries who created "a more perfect union." Passage of the Fifteenth Amendment elevated African-American men to a political status that thrust them into the patriarchal world. White women remained on their pedestals, cherished positions to be revered and envied. African-American women had once again been omitted from the cornerstone of American democracy, the Constitution of the United States. There was a difference made in 1870, however: She was no longer to be counted as three-fifths of a person; she was zero.

REFERENCES

Bennett, Lerone. 1964. *Before the Mayflower: A History of the Negro in America, 1619-1964*. Baltimore: Penguin Books.

Catt, Carrie Chapman, and Nettie Rogers Shuler. 1969. *Woman Suffrage and Politics*. Seattle: University of Washington Press.

Davis, Angela. 1971. "The Black Woman's Role in the Community of Slaves." *The Black Scholar* 2:3-14.

Dred Scott v. Sandford. 1857. 60 U.S. 19 Howard 393 (1857).

DuBois, Ellen Carol. 1987. "Outgrowing the Compact of the Fathers: Equal Rights, Woman Suffrage, and the United States Constitution, 1820-1878." *The Journal of American History* 74:836-862.

Elliott, Ward E. Y. 1974. *The Rise of Guardian Democracy: The Supreme Court's Role in Voting Rights Disputes, 1845-1869*. Cambridge: Harvard University Press.

Fishel, Leslie Jr., and Benjamin Quarles. 1970. *The Black American: A Documentary History*. Glenview, IL: Scott, Foresman and Company.

Hine, Darlene, and Kate Wittenstein. 1981. "Female Slave Resistance: The Economics of Sex." In *The Black Woman Cross-Culturally*, ed. Filomina Chioma Steady. Boston: Schenkman.

Hofstadter, Richard. 1948. *The American Political Tradition*. New York: Vintage Books.

Hooks, Bell. 1981. *Ain't I a Woman: Black Women and Feminism*. Boston: South End Press.

Horton, James Oliver. 1986. "Freedom's Yoke: Gender Conventions Among Antebellum Free Blacks." *Feminist Studies* 12:51-76.

Hurston, Zora Neale. 1969. *Their Eyes Were Watching God*. New York: Negro Universities Press.

Lobel, Jules. 1987. "The Constitution and American Radicalism." *Social Policy* 18:20-23.

Madison, James. 1961. "Federalist 54." In Alexander Hamilton, James Madison, and John Jay, *The Federalist Papers*, ed. Clinton Rossiter. New York: New American Library. (Original work published in 1788.)

Marshall, Thurgood. 1987. "Justice Thurgood Marshall's Remarks on the Bicentennial of the U.S. Constitution." *Signs* 13:2-6.

Papachristou, Judith. 1976. *Women Together: A History in Documents of the Women's Movement in the United States*. New York: Alfred A. Knopf.

Stanton, Elizabeth Cady. 1970. "This Is the Negro's Hour." In *Voices From Women's Liberation*, ed. Leslie B. Tanner. New York: Signet Books.

Stewart, Maria. 1973. "What If I Am a Woman?" In *Black Women in White America*, ed. Gerda Lerner. New York: Vintage Books.

Terborg-Penn, Rosalyn. 1981. "Discrimination Against Afro-American Women in the Women's Movement, 1830-1920." In *The Black Woman Cross-Culturally*, ed. Filomina Chioma Steady. Cambridge, MA: Schenkman.

Truth, Sojourner. 1973. "I Suppose I Am About the Only Colored Woman That Goes About to Speak for the Rights of Colored Women." In *Black Women in White America*, ed. Gerda Lerner. New York: Vintage Books.

Weld, Angelina Grimke. 1970. "The Rights of Women and Negroes." In *Voices From Women's Liberation*, ed. Leslie B. Tanner. New York: Signet Books.

Female Suffrage in New Jersey, 1790-1807

Irwin N. Gertzog

SUMMARY. Conventional descriptions of how New Jersey women secured the right to vote in the late eighteenth century, and of the extent to which they took advantage of that right, tend to be incomplete. Moreover, the subsequent disenfranchisement of women was not principally a product of corruption in an 1807 Essex County referendum, as some maintain, as much as it was a result of a shift in the balance of power within the state.

The fact that women voted in New Jersey during the post-Revolutionary-War period is not widely known and, among those who are aware of it, not sufficiently appreciated. History texts sometimes make fleeting references to it, and studies of voting in the United States treat it as a peculiar and unimportant aberration. Few attempt to explain or even to describe the circumstances under which women secured the right to vote, the frequency with which eligible women went to the polls, or the reasons for which the state legislature later repealed women's suffrage. (See, for example, Porter 1918, and Williamson 1960.)

This article is a partial summary of a larger study of women voters in New Jersey during the late eighteenth and early nineteenth centuries. It addresses the three questions alluded to above. First, why did New Jersey confer the franchise on women in the late eighteenth century, when by all indications there was not another state in the union even considering taking such a step? Second, once given the vote, to what extent did eligible women make use of it?

Irwin N. Gertzog is affiliated with Allegheny College.

And, third, what circumstances prompted New Jersey lawmakers to disenfranchise women in 1807?

ENFRANCHISING NEW JERSEY WOMEN

Most explanations of why New Jersey women were given the vote in the post-Revolution period are linked to two central facts. The first is that the New Jersey constitution of 1776 contained an unusually permissive suffrage provision. The second is that an influential Quaker lawmaker who believed in the equality of women was able successfully to impose his egalitarian values on his colleagues in the state legislature.

The 1776 New Jersey constitution conferred the vote on "all inhabitants" who met specified property and residence requirements. No prohibition was imposed explicitly on women residents who satisfied the property requirement ("50 pounds clear estate"), and nothing in the document limited the vote to males. In short, the constitution was silent with respect to the relationship between gender and voting rights.

One reason for the constitutional convention's use of so broad an expression as "all inhabitants" is that delegates were pressured to employ it by New Jersey citizens who, until then, had been unable to satisfy more proscriptive eligibility requirements. Many of these residents were expected in the months ahead to provide much of the money and manpower needed to end British rule through the force of arms. By using the phrase "all inhabitants," the framers of the constitution were sending a signal to the men who would finance and fight the war that the new state was prepared to be generous in the distribution of political rights. Wider public support for the new constitution and for the Revolution was expected in return (Erdman 1929, 31-32; Pole 1956, 189; Turner 1916, 166-167).

Another explanation for the permissive language is that the delegates meeting in New Brunswick did not have the time to fashion more specific restrictive terminology. The convention was itself an act of rebellion, and its participants had already ordered the arrest of the colonial governor. When word reached the New Brunswick conferees, at the end of June 1776, that General Howe and his British forces had anchored off New Jersey's Sandy Hook, they feared that the British army might force them to end their convention before a constitution could be drafted. In the face of this military threat, the rebels hurried their work and adopted a document that failed to incorporate details that a more deliberative body would almost certainly have demanded (Erdman 1929, 47; Turner 1916, 166).

These explanations would be more persuasive if New Jersey had been the only state whose first constitution neither limited the vote to men nor explicitly excluded women. In fact, the constitutions and laws of several of the 13 original states were similarly silent on the relationship between gender and the franchise (Porter 1918, 20). Political leaders in these states, and perhaps in New Jersey as well, apparently assumed that it was unnecessary to prohibit female suffrage. They seem to have concluded that, since women were not eligible to vote prior to the Revolution, no one would expect them to vote after the attainment of independence. As we now know, these expectations were borne out in all states save New Jersey.

There is little evidence that women voted in the years immediately following the Revolution, but when the legislature revised its election law in 1790 the phrase "he or she" was incorporated to refer to eligible voters. The credit for effecting this change is generally given to Joseph Cooper, a lawmaker from Gloucester County. Cooper was a Quaker, a member of a religious sect that had a significant following in a territory once known as "West Jersey." At the time, that region consisted of Cape May, Hunterdon, Cumberland, Burlington, and Salem counties, in addition to Gloucester, and it generally constituted an area that we know today as southern New Jersey. Quakers made up the most numerous religious sect in the last three of these counties, and the conservative economic and political orientations of its devotees dominated most of that region (Pasler and Pasler 1969, 198-199).

Quaker doctrine with respect to the role of women in religious life, however, was decidedly untraditional. Unlike virtually all other religious groups in the country at that time, the Quakers believed in some measure of political and social equality between men and women, and Cooper seems to have held this view as fervently as any of his coreligionists.

It has been said that the Gloucester County lawmaker was a

member of the legislative committee appointed to draft what became the 1790 Election Law, and that he used his position on the panel, along with the high regard in which he was held, to persuade colleagues to recognize the valuable contribution that women could make to society and to the state. Accordingly, female suffrage in New Jersey has been attributed to the influence of the large number of Quaker residents within its boundaries, along with the leadership of Joseph Cooper (Pole 1953, 52-53; Turner 1916, 168; Whitehead 1858, 102).

An investigation into Cooper's role in passing the Election Law and into the circumstances under which the phrase "he or she" was inserted into the Law suggests that the conventional account of these events is at least partly incorrect and almost certainly incomplete. In the first place, Cooper, although a member of the legislature at the time, was not a member of the committee that drafted and reported out the Election Law (McCormick 1953, 93). It is true that Cooper authored an important election statute that was passed in 1797, and it is also true that the 1790 measure was introduced by a Quaker from Gloucester County. But Cooper was not the sponsor of the 1790 measure, and there is no evidence that he was the driving force behind its adoption. Second, appealing though it may be to attribute egalitarian motives to those who helped New Jersey women secure the vote, there seems to be a more compelling explanation for female suffrage than the one offered in the few sources that explore the subject. This interpretation has its roots in the bitter political battle that took place the year before, during the winter and spring of 1789, when New Jersey was selecting its Representatives to the first United States Congress. The state legislature declared that the four New Jersey seats in the U.S. House of Representatives would be chosen at large, rather than from single-member districts. Accordingly, a group of conservatives—most of them businessmen, many of them Quakers, a large majority of them from the southern counties, and all of them destined to be members of the Federalist Party—organized a slate of candidates that reflected their sponsors' economic, partisan, and regional preferences. This slate came to be referred to as the "Junto" ticket (McCormick 1949, 242).

The tactics employed by those who crafted and supported the

Junto ticket included, first of all, gaining control of the election process in the southern counties and keeping the polls there open for weeks beyond their customary closing dates. Given the considerable length of time that it took many residents to travel to election sites, polls were often open for two or more days. However, Junto sponsors went well beyond the accepted practices of the period to ensure that voters sympathetic to their House candidates would have sufficient time to cast their ballots.

Second, they awaited the election results from the northern counties before counting votes recorded in the southern counties so that they could determine how large a margin the Junto ticket would be required to overcome in order to carry the state (McCormick 1949, 244). Third, they arranged subsequently to have the state legislature ignore the vote count from Essex County, an opposition stronghold, which had kept its polls open for an even longer period of time than Junto politicos had managed to get away with—accepting votes from February 11 to April 27 (McCormick 1949, 247).

These events must surely have influenced the state legislature when it convened the next year to consider a new election law. The measure that was finally adopted limited the number of days during which polls could be kept open and prescribed the manner in which votes should be counted. But the lawmakers, a majority of whom apparently possessed the same conservative, proto-Federalist preferences that had fueled the Junto victory in 1789, did not confine their attention to election machinery. They also conferred the vote on those women who could meet residence and property requirements. However, while adopting the phrase "he or she" when referring to potential voters, they limited the reach of the entire statute to only seven of the 13 counties. Four of the seven contained the highest concentration of Quaker residents, and all seven boasted considerable, if not overwhelming, incipient Federalist Party strength. The lawmakers also provided for establishment of polling places in each township within the seven counties, thereby assuring greater turnout in them than in the remaining six, where voting sites were less numerous and less accessible (Acts of the 15th New Jersey General Assembly, November 18, 1790, 670).

Apparently these legislators reasoned that, if they were to continue to win elections in the future, women, an element of the population that until then had been disfranchised, would need to be granted the right to vote in those counties in which loyalty to conservative principles was an article of faith. The remaining six counties, some of which were already showing radical, Jeffersonian predilections, would thus be forced to overcome – with the votes of males alone – the numerical advantage that conservative candidates would secure from both male and female supporters in the seven heavily Federalist counties.

Thus the egalitarian motives alleged to have prompted Quakers and others to confer the vote on New Jersey women were probably less important in achieving that result than the struggle for economic and political power within the state.

FEMALE VOTER TURNOUT

Just how often women voted in elections after 1790 is difficult to determine. Some believe that female turnout was generally light (Dinkin 1982, 42; Prince 1967, 134). On the other hand, many scholars distinguish between the years preceding and those following 1797, the year in which an election law extended the vote to women in the six counties that were unaffected by the earlier statute; they maintain that from 1790 to 1797 female turnout was barely perceptible (McCormick 1953, 78; Pole 1953, 44; Whitehead 1858, 102). Several scholars point out that, because women did not actively seek the vote, they were disinclined to take the trouble to go to the polls once they had received it. Supporters of this view base their conclusion on the observation that newspapers of the period made little or no mention of women's election day activities. A high turnout, these historians reason, would certainly have occasioned explicit press coverage (Pole 1953, 44; Turner 1916, 170).

They could be right, of course, but the newspaper accounts upon which they tend to rely were published in counties that had not yet extended the vote to women – Essex and Middlesex counties, for example. Publications appearing in, say, Burlington and Gloucester counties before 1797 are not cited by those who have studied female suffrage during this period.

Most of these same commentators agree, however, that following passage of the 1797 Act women began to appear at the polls in considerable numbers (Pole 1953, 53; Turner 1916, 186). Frequent allusion is made to an item in the Newark *Centinel of Freedom* estimating that 75 women in the (then) Essex County community of Elizabeth voted in the 1797 state legislative contest. Later, the Trenton *True American* reported that female turnout rose to "alarming heights" in the election of 1802, possibly making up as much as 25% of the total vote cast.

This increase in female participation is explained as a product of the feverish get-out-the-vote drives by emerging political parties (Pole 1953, 59). By the late 1790s, fledgling Federalist and Jeffersonian Republican Party organizations had begun to appear and contests for office had become more competitive. According to many who have written about this period, both parties increased their efforts to capture the women's vote (Griffith 1799, 33; Pole 1953, 53; Whitehead 1858, 103). Thus the parties are portrayed as opportunistic, and women voters are viewed as willing, mindless pawns—characteristics rarely attributed by these commentators to males, many of whose electoral choices seem to have been dictated by the people by whom they were employed (Pasler and Pasler 1969, 198-199).

It seems reasonable to conclude that women probably voted as frequently as one might expect any newly enfranchised group of people to vote—people not yet accustomed to participating in elections. Moreover, turnout apparently was affected by the same legal and political factors that normally influence the participation of any aggregation of would-be voters: More women tended to go to the polls when contests were hotly contested, when counties had more polling sites, when voting was by secret ballot rather than open declaration of preference, and when more important offices were at stake. Thus, newspapers reported a heavy female turnout for the 1800 Presidential election, with Jeffersonian Republicans celebrating the role of New Jersey women in that contest even though their candidate had not carried the state (*Centinel of Freedom*, March 17, 1801). An unexciting 1807 legislative contest in one Burlington County community saw women make up only 12% of the total vote (De Cou 1929, 50).

These proportions may seem small, but New Jersey women of the period were forced to confront several important deterrents to voter participation. One involved the manner in which they were forced to cast their votes. Many counties chose officials by voice vote, and most polling places were located in taverns. This meant that a woman who had not had much experience with politics would have to go to a tavern alive with men in high spirits and, in the presence of candidates buying drinks for potential supporters, announce her choices (Pasler 1964, 53-54). This must surely have been a daunting experience even for the most determined women. In fact, the order in which names appear on the few available voting lists of the period suggests that women came to the polls in groups, thereby providing one another with the psychic support and the courage to announce their candidate preferences in what must often have been an unsavory setting.

Whatever the proportion of women who made use of the franchise, most historians have concluded that they did not object to the loss of their voting rights (McCormick 1953, 98-99; Turner 1916, 185). This inference is based, in part, on the fact that women did not insert items in the newspapers to decry the injustices of the 1807 Election Act. The claim is further justified by the observation that memorials from women to the state legislature demanding reinstatement of female suffrage were conspicuous by their absence. But the fact that women's names rarely appeared as authors of *any* newspaper items, and the fact that petitions and memorials to the state legislature seldom bore women's names except in connection with a few circumscribed issues—requests for divorce, for example (Kerber 1986, 87)—make these inferences questionable.

DISENFRANCHISING NEW JERSEY WOMEN

Historians tend to agree about the reasons why women were deprived of the right to vote in 1807. Most suggest that the public grew increasingly dissatisfied with the frequency with which one or the other of the political parties tried to exploit women by "herding" them to the polls, where they were perceived to cast their votes mindlessly for candidates about whom they knew virtually nothing (McCormick 1953, 99). Added to this growing irritation was the occurrence in 1807 of a corrupt referendum in Essex County in which women were said to have played a visibly ignoble part (Prince 1967, 134).

The referendum pitted the residents of Elizabeth against those of Newark in determining the location of the county seat. It seems that Essex County needed a new courthouse and jail, and each of its two largest communities vied for a site within or near its own boundaries. When county officials could not agree on which of the two to favor, they persuaded the state legislature to authorize a referendum so that the citizenry of the entire county could decide the issue (Turner 1916, 181).

The voting took place over a three-day period, with the polls established first in Springfield for a day, then moved to Elizabeth for a day, and finally set up in Newark for the final day of balloting. Residents of the contending communities shamelessly moved from site to site and voted at each, sometimes cloaked in a disguise. It was reported that male youths, dressed as women, cast multiple ballots, and that both men and women were guilty of registering their choices on two or more occasions. A few darkened their faces with charcoal and voted in the guise of free blacks (Prince 1967, 134; Turner 1916, 182).

When the ballots were counted, Newark had won, but the total numbers of votes recorded in some precincts were suspiciously, even outrageously, high. In Newark, where 1,600 people had voted in the election of 1806, 5,000 ballots were cast in the referendum a few months later. In the town of Springfield, 300 people had voted in the preceding legislative contest and more than 2,400 votes were recorded in the referendum. The fraud was so palpable that the state legislature eventually threw out the result (Turner 1916, 183).

According to most published accounts, the drive for reform was now irresistible. In October 1807, the legislature limited the vote to "free, white, male citizens" 21 years of age (Acts of the 32nd New Jersey General Assembly, November 16, 1807, 14). All at once, state lawmakers had disenfranchised free blacks, noncitizens, and women in an action that they believed was justified by the need to rationalize the administration of elections and to reduce political corruption. That most of the illegal activities associated with the referendum had been engaged in by white males seems not to have mattered. What was important to lawmakers was that the potential voting power of three "easily manipulated" and marginal groups should not be abused by unscrupulous elements of the white, male majority. And the way to resolve the problem was simply to deny members of these groups the right to vote.

But, like the conventional explanation for how New Jersey women secured the franchise in 1790, this account, too, is incomplete. The need for election reform was certainly highlighted by misdeeds in the Essex County referendum. But several fundamental changes had taken place within New Jersey since 1790, and these changes altered the distribution of power within the state. In 1801, the Jeffersonian Republicans replaced the Federalists as New Jersey's dominant political party, and the locus of power moved to the more populous northern counties (Pasler and Pasler 1974). In 1804, the legislature voted to free the slaves within the state on a gradual basis; since the great majority of slaves resided in the northern counties, that region stood to increase significantly its voting power vis-à-vis the southern counties.

Since many of the northern Jeffersonian Republicans had never been comfortable with women's suffrage, and since southern conservative Federalists were probably fearful that the much larger number of northern voters would be swelled further by an increase in black voters, legislators from both regions agreed to strip the vote from both groups.

Even if southern legislators had not been party to this possibly inexplicit bargain among lawmakers, the disenfranchisement of women would almost certainly have occurred before long, for what was happening in New Jersey cannot be isolated from similar developments in other states. By the beginning of the nineteenth century, almost all states were extending the vote to larger and larger proportions of white males. At the same time, however, state after state took steps legally to deny that privilege to their marginal populations. Virtually every northern state disenfranchised free blacks and aliens (Wesley 1947, 154). For women, a return to second-class citizenship occurred only in New Jersey, because they had never been empowered to vote in any other state.

CONCLUSION

In sum, women were given the vote in 1790 less because of the egalitarian spirit characteristic of Quakerism than because of the clash of economic, partisan, and regional forces and the struggle for political control of the state. Once they got the vote, women were not simply hustled to the polls when signaled to do so in order to support predesignated candidates; they seem to have responded to the same political forces that motivated males. When polls were readily accessible, when elections were closely contested, and when the stakes were high, they turned out.

Later, they lost the vote not so much because a few (out of a weakness believed to be common to their sex) had engaged in illegal behavior in an Essex County referendum; they were deprived of the vote largely because, as women, unable to hold public office and forbidden by the norms of the period from resorting to tactics fostering political mobilization, they could not protect themselves from a resourceful majority who wanted to reform the election process and believed that it was in their own interests to disenfranchise politically marginal groups.

REFERENCES

Acts of the 15th New Jersey General Assembly. November 18, 1790.

Acts of the 32nd New Jersey General Assembly. November 16, 1807.

De Cou, G. 1929. *Moorestown and Her Neighbors*.

Dinkin, Robert J. 1982. *Voting in Revolutionary America: A Study of Elections in the Original Thirteen States, 1776-1789*. Westport, CT: Greenwood Press.

Erdman, C. R. 1929. *The New Jersey Constitution of 1776*.

Griffith, W. 1799. *Eumenes*.

Kerber, Linda K. 1986. *Women of the Republic: Intellect and Ideology in Revolutionary America*. Chapel Hill, NC: The University of North Carolina Press.

McCormick, Richard P. 1949. "New Jersey's First Congressional Election, 1789: A Case Study in Political Skulduggery." *The William and Mary Quarterly* series 3, no. 6.

McCormick, Richard P. 1953. *The History of Voting in New Jersey: A Study of the Development of Election Machinery, 1664-1911*.

Pasler, Rudolph J. 1964. "The Federalist Party in Burlington County, New Jersey." Master's thesis. University of Delaware.

Pasler, Rudolph J., and Margaret C. Pasler. Winter 1969. "Federalist Tenacity in Burlington County, 1810-1824." *New Jersey History* 87:197-210.

Pasler, Rudolph J., and Margaret C. Pasler. 1974. *The New Jersey Federalists*. Rutherford, NJ: Fairleigh Dickinson University Press.

Pole, J. R. 1953. "The Suffrage in New Jersey, 1790-1807." *Proceedings of the New Jersey Historical Society*.

Pole, J. R. July 1956. "Suffrage Reform and the American Revolution in New Jersey." *Proceedings of the New Jersey Historical Society* 74:173-194.

Porter, Kirk H. 1918. *History of Suffrage in the United States*. Westport, CT: Greenwood Press.

Prince, Carl E. 1967. *New Jersey's Jeffersonian Republicans: The Genesis of an Early Party Machine, 1789-1817*. Chapel Hill, NC: University of North Carolina Press.

Turner, E. R. 1916. "Women's Suffrage in New Jersey: 1790-1807." *Smith College Studies in History* 1(4).

Wesley, Charles H. 1947. "Negro Suffrage in the Period of Constitution-Making, 1787-1865." *The Journal of Negro History* 32:143-168.

Whitehead, W. A. 1858. "A Brief Statement of the Facts Connected With the Origin, Practice and Prohibition of Female Suffrage in New Jersey." *Proceedings of the New Jersey Historical Society* series 1, no. 8.

Williamson, C. 1960. *American Suffrage: From Property to Democracy, 1760-1860*.

The Significance of the Nineteenth Amendment: A New Look at Civil Rights, Social Welfare, and Woman Suffrage Alignments in the Progressive Era

Eileen Lorenzi McDonagh

SUMMARY. The significance of the Nineteenth Amendment for contemporary gender gap politics, and for its own Progressive Era time period, is investigated by analyzing votes for woman suffrage in the House of Representatives in relation to civil rights, civil liberties, and social welfare legislation. A major conclusion is that the woman suffrage issue was connected to civil rights concerns for the duration of its legislative history, which seriously calls into question the interpretation of the "expediency" thesis, which claims the primarily instrumental value of enfranchising women for the sake of "status consistency" goals.

The significance of the Nineteenth Amendment enfranchising women is evident today in the arenas of power politics and aca-

---

Eileen Lorenzi McDonagh is affiliated with Radcliffe College and Northeastern University.

The author gratefully acknowledges the helpful advice of Mary Katzenstein, Sidney Verba, Debra Kaufman, Carol Mueller, and the research assistance of Edward Price.

This research is supported by National Science Foundation Grant R11-880499 and by The Henry A. Murray Research Center of Radcliffe College. Acknowledgment is extended to the Inter-University Consortium for Political and Social Research for providing some of the data used in this research; neither the original source nor collectors of the data nor the Consortium bear any responsibility for the analyses or interpretations presented here.

demic scholarship. In practical politics, it is this most fundamental of all political rights—the right to vote—that is a key condition making possible contemporary "gender gap" politics and empowering women as political participants at the elite level of campaigns and candidacies as well as at the grass-roots level of active partisan voters.

In addition, one of the promises of the earlier woman suffrage campaign—to infuse the public sphere of politics with the values associated with the private sphere of the family—seems more incorporated into our political culture now than ever before. The media's cornucopian display of personal familial relationships in the context of defining contemporary political candidates testifies to the merging of the personal and the political. Similarly, support by today's presidential candidates for such social policy issues as day care reflects the adoption of issues related to family roles located in the "private sphere" of the home as legitimate agenda items for the "public sphere" epitomized by national presidential politics.

Though recent memories usually date the slogan, "the personal is political," to the 1960s, it is argued here that a more accurate historical locus for this phrase, and for concomitant accomplishments in advancing issues that are of particular import to women, is the Progressive Era. It was in the course of moving the issue of woman suffrage from the state to the national level, in the final successful drive to pass an amendment to the federal Constitution, that the demands to connect the personal and the political as well as to attend to specific legislative policies related to women's needs were forcefully declared. Attention to the significance of the Nineteenth Amendment brings to light the continuity of the heritage linking reform movements of the 1960s with the earlier 1900-1920 reform decades of the Progressive Era.

The significance of the Nineteenth Amendment also figures prominently in current academic scholarship. Following the wake of an almost hostile neglect of woman suffrage, contemporary research is drawing attention to women's political accomplishments in the 1920s as virtually the prototypical model of feminist political activity.[1] In Nancy F. Cott's most recent evaluation (1987), the campaign for woman suffrage is an example par excellence of how "the focus on the ballot . . . enabled groups of very different women to build coalitions toward a common goal . . . [and how the] vote harmonized the two strands . . . 'sameness' and 'difference' arguments, 'justice' and 'expediency' arguments . . . [encompassing] the broadest spectrum of ideas and participants" (Cott 1987, 7, 30).

Thus, according to Cott's analysis, the fundamental characteristic of feminism is a basic plurality of interests due to the heterogeneity of women as a group. The suffrage campaign is significant for its successful unification of these diverse interests in the drive to achieve passage of a national amendment enfranchising women.

Kristi Andersen's recent work evaluates the problematic low levels of political participation among women after enfranchisement in terms of the very unique "learning" problems involved. Chief among the decisions to be made was not only which party to support but whether women's political mobilization should entail any partisan allegiance at all. In addition, the literature is growing that reevaluates the voting patterns of women after passage of the Nineteenth Amendment in terms of longitudinal turnout declines rather than in terms of a passive orientation on the part of newly enfranchised women voters. The conclusion is that the poor turnout among women voters of the 1920s is best understood in the context of longitudinal voting trends rather than assumptions about women's political potential per se (Kleppner 1982).

Mary F. Katzenstein (1984) underscores the recent "rediscovery" of the importance of the vote, and of electoral politics, for feminism, noting that "there have been good reasons . . . for feminism's indifference to or skepticism about the power of the vote. But there are even better reasons why we must appreciate both its past importance and future potential" (6).

Finally, the point has been made recently by Carol Mueller that the absence of media coverage of polling and political participation rates of men and women in the 1920s not only makes it highly problematic to quantify women's contribution to electoral politics in the 1920s but also means that important sources for the very creation of today's "gender gap" simply did not exist during that earlier time period (Mueller 1988).

The implication of the new scholarship cited above for reestablishing the significance of the Nineteenth Amendment is twofold. First, rather than merely representing a formal, legal accomplishment gained by the efforts of a small middle-class-bound sector of American women, the Nineteenth Amendment became the law of the land as the result of a consolidation of a plurality of diverse political interests. As such, the Nineteenth Amendment is viewed as the crucial accomplishment initiating women as full political citizens, upon which status the feminist activism of today depends.

Second, the disappointments centering on women's low turnout after passage of the Nineteenth Amendment are now viewed more accurately as a result of structural factors, over which women had no control, rather than as a basis for questioning the intrinsic value of the Nineteenth Amendment or the inherent nature of American women as active political participants. As noted above, the most important of these structural factors now receiving scholarly attention are the partisan dilemmas faced by women, the lack of public opinion polls and instruments necessary to publicize women's potential voting bloc power, and demographic trends falsely attributing to women full responsibility for the unusually low turnout patterns that were characteristic of the 1920s in general.

In addition to a renewed appreciation of the significance of the Nineteenth Amendment for today's politics and scholarship, evaluation of the Nineteenth Amendment casts its own time period, the Progressive Era, in a new light. Often regarded as decades of conflicting, if not chaotic, reform orientations (Filene 1970), the early period of the twentieth century can be assessed anew by focusing on the woman suffrage issue in the context of other civil rights and social welfare legislation considered during the 1900-1920 period. The Nineteenth Amendment provides a powerful analytic perspective of its own time period because of the issue complexity characterizing the arguments for and against woman suffrage. To get at this complexity, we will focus on woman suffrage in the specific context of legislative activity.

Woman suffrage campaigns have received invaluable study as social movements, as lobbying interest group phenomena, and as vehicles for biographical treatment of major suffrage leaders. However, it is critical to remember first and foremost that the drive for woman suffrage rested on a legislative goal: passage of laws enfranchising women, first at the state and then at the national level.

Leadership, lobbying activities, and the coalescing of groups to form social movements to achieve these legislative goals are all of fundamental importance for understanding the accomplishments of the suffrage campaign. However, in the final analysis, the ultimate test of success for woman suffrage efforts was the passage of legislation itself.

This research, therefore, analyzes voting patterns supporting and opposing woman suffrage in the federal Congress. It is these voting patterns that ultimately empowered women as full political citizens and that also reveal the actual issue connections between woman suffrage and the civil rights and social welfare legislation of the Progressive Era. The ensuing analysis of voting patterns in the national Congress complements the invaluable groundwork laid by studies of how suffrage got to the national congressional agenda in the first place and adds important clarification of issue alignments at the level of actual voting patterns in the national Congress.

WOMAN SUFFRAGE: ISSUE CONNECTIONS

Scholarship to date has depicted the woman suffrage issue in a number of conflicting ways. First, there is the important Aileen Kraditor thesis that argues that at the turn of the century the campaign for women's rights was based almost exclusively on expediency arguments stressing the utilitarian values of admitting women to complete participating status in the polity (Kraditor 1965). Chief among such utilities was the promise that women would bring into the electorate "educated, responsible" female voters who could counterbalance what was assumed to be the threatening, if not destructive, impact of newly enfranchised "uneducated, irresponsible" immigrant and black male voters.

In this interpretation, not only does the expediency argument replace earlier "rights and justice" arguments for woman suffrage, but these utilitarian principles become associated with what can only (distressingly) be labeled as racist arguments for woman suffrage. An example of the rhetoric, if not logic, associated with this view of woman suffrage is captured in the following resolution passed by the National American Woman Suffrage Association (NAWSA) at its convention in Washington, D.C., in 1893:

> *Resolved*. That without expressing any opinion on the proper qualifications for voting, we call attention to the significant facts that in every State there are more women who can read and write than the whole number of illiterate male voters; more white women who can read and write than all negro voters; more American women who can read and write than all foreign voters; so that the enfranchisement of such women would settle the vexed question of rule by illiteracy, whether of home-grown or foreign-born production. (Buhle and Buhle 1978, 328)

Such arguments about the political power of adding women's vote to the electorate as a way of neutralizing the "unwanted" impact of immigrant and black (male) votes were made even more explicit in appeals to enfranchise women in the South, the one region where woman suffrage barely mustered any support at all. In the words of Belle Kearney in her address to the NAWSA in 1903, "the enfranchisement of women would insure immediate and durable white supremacy, honestly attained, for upon unquestioned authority it is stated that in every southern State but one there are more educated women than all the illiterate voters, white and black, native and foreign, combined. . . . The South is slow to grasp the great fact that the enfranchisement of women would settle the race question in politics. . . . The South [will] be compelled to look to its Anglo-Saxon women as the medium through which to retain the supremacy of the white race over the African" (Buhle and Buhle 1978, 348-349).

Record has it that Miss Kearney's speech was received enthusiastically by those attending the NAWSA convention that she addressed, and the above quotes exemplify why many historians to date have associated the woman suffrage issue with "expediency," if not with racist orientations. However, we will be examining the degree to which such issue connections operated at the level of voting patterns on legislation in the national Congress. Did House members who supported woman suffrage also support such legislation as immigration restriction and denial of black rights? Put another way, can we discern in the congressional roll-call voting patterns support and opposition to the woman suffrage amendment related to such racist orientations?

The focus on utilitarian arguments proffered by some leaders of the woman suffrage movement places the Nineteenth Amendment in the same issue domain as another major legislative battle of the Progressive Era: prohibition. The Eighteenth Amendment, prohibiting the manufacture, sale, transportation, import, and export of all intoxicating liquors, was ratified in 1919 just a little more than a year prior to the ratification of the Nineteenth Amendment enfranchising women. Even more significant than this juxtaposition in time, however, is the long history linking these two pieces of legislation.

At the level of social movement leadership, the earlier temperance campaigns of the nineteenth century provided many women with their first experiences in political organization, which later served them well as the woman suffrage organizations emerged as a distinct and separate concern. The leadership overlap between woman suffrage and temperance organizations bolstered a public perception of a connection between these two issues. The perception was deeply reinforced by liquor interests prophesying that a vote for woman suffrage would be a vote for prohibition. Intensive campaigning by liquor interests to prevent passage of prohibition legislation—and, instrumentally, to prevent passage of woman suffrage legislation—produced at the very least a legacy in which there was a perceived connection between these two legislative goals. Furthermore, this connection is affirmed in just about every historical account of these two issues.[2]

However, again our question focuses on the actual voting patterns on prohibition and woman suffrage in the national Congress where legislators are empowered to enact laws. If prohibition and woman suffrage are linked, do we find House members supporting both and opposing both, as historians' accounts would lead us to expect? Despite the attention directed to prohibition and woman suffrage as social movements, there has been little analysis of how lobbying tactics translated into actual congressional voting patterns on these issues.

The expediency arguments cited above suggest a congruity of woman suffrage, prohibition, and immigration and racial issue positions. In this formulation, the chief value entailed in the enfranchisement of women is the provision of new votes instrumental for social and political control of the behavior of such "undesired" groups as immigrants and blacks. We want to suggest that this formulation, if correct, would involve not only a transformation of woman suffrage, from a civil rights issue in the nineteenth century to an instrumental expediency issue in the twentieth, but also the metamorphosis of woman suffrage from a positive civil rights issue for women to a negative civil rights issue for immigrants and blacks.

If the Kraditor thesis is correct—and that, of course, is the question—we argue here that civil rights and civil liberties principles are intimately involved in so-called expediency and status consistency goals. We argue this because the goal of social control in the case of prohibition, for example, was not one of regulation but rather one of an absolute and universal legal ban on the use of all alcoholic beverages. This legal ban, established at the level of a constitutional amendment, bypassed all intermediate forms of regulation such as monitoring conditions of sale, education about consumption, and rehabilitation of substance abusers. Instead, prohibition legislation was as absolute and universal as legally possible, denying both the right and the liberty of individuals to partake of any alcoholic beverage under any conditions, despite the presence of large populations whose life-styles—including religious ceremonies—had traditionally involved such substances for centuries.

The repeal of the Eighteenth Amendment suggests not only the practical failure entailed in its implementation but also the original distortion involved in its formulation. It was not merely a regulatory issue involving "social control" but an infringement of the individual rights and liberties of American citizens. As such, prohibition needs to be classified as a "negative civil rights and civil liberties" issue, and any alignment it might have had with woman suffrage is clearly problematic, not merely from the standpoint of instrumental expediency but also from the standpoint of the heritage of woman suffrage as a civil rights issue in its own right.[3]

Thus the definition of prohibition as a civil rights, civil liberties issue, along with what has been its assumed relationship to woman suffrage, raises some serious questions about the nature of the woman suffrage issue in the Progressive Era. The seriousness of these questions is only more evident in the context of the racist element involved in expediency logic, as cited above. Did the view that woman suffrage was a means to accomplish "white supremacy" translate into a connection between support for woman suffrage and support for negative civil rights legislation in the national Congress? This question will be examined by analyzing patterns of support for woman suffrage in the House of Representatives in relation to voting patterns on such negative civil rights legislation as the prohibition of interracial marriage in the District of Columbia and the ban on all black and African immigration. In this way the Kraditor thesis is extended by asking not merely whether woman suffrage had become an expediency issue by 1900 but whether, in fact, classification as an expediency issue in this time period invokes basic civil rights and civil liberties issue positions as well.

Equally important to the above analysis, however, is the attachment of the woman suffrage issue to the innovative social welfare and social justice legislation of its time period. Another potential promise embedded in the rhetoric of suffrage leaders seeking to garner support for enfranchising women was the claim that women would add to the public sphere of politics what researchers today would call the "emotion-work" and "caring-work" most often associated with the private sphere of the family (Ostrander 1989).

This was a powerful argument in these early decades of the twentieth century when government was just beginning to be called upon to take responsibility for the welfare needs of individuals. The association of women with a concern for such needs—as well as the enfranchisement of women in order to increase the number of voters supportive of such governmental policies—contributed not only to the very origin of the welfare state, but also to the way its initial implementation was envisioned.

The importance of women's contribution of this caring, if not maternal, orientation to the public sphere was most apparent, perhaps, in regard to legislation designed to restrict child labor. Though child labor legislation failed as a constitutional amendment, it nevertheless was of salient concern to legislators during the Progressive Era. Women's involvement and concern about this issue was one example of how the enfranchising of women was viewed as an important way of adding to the electorate a huge group of voters who would push for and support such basic social welfare legislation as child labor restriction.

Women's commitment to labor legislation in general remained more problematic, due to some conflict of interest between labor union goals and women's labor concerns. Nevertheless, the general belief in women's inherent sensitivity and commitment to the social welfare of human beings—that is, women's maternal, nurturing character—was viewed by many during this time as a prime reason for getting women into the electorate (or for keeping them out, depending on one's orientation toward social welfare legislation).

Thus, we see two very different bases for assessing the significance of the woman suffrage issue in the Progressive Era. On the one hand, we interpret expediency arguments for woman suffrage legislation as linking it with the attempt to constrict politically the exercise of civil liberties and civil rights of immigrants and blacks. According to our analysis, the social control goals involved in immigration restriction and prohibition legislation went beyond mere regulatory concerns. Rather, such legislation embodied the negation of basic civil rights and civil liberties of the target groups involved. If woman suffrage is linked as an instrumental means to negate the civil rights and civil liberties of "unwanted" elements in the American political system—and that remains a prime question—then Kraditor's thesis takes on new import. Suffrage becomes not merely an expediency issue by the turn of the century but, rather, an issue dramatically changing from an embodiment of positive civil rights in the nineteenth century to one meant to implement negative civil rights legislation in the twentieth century.

On the other hand, women were viewed during the Progressive Era as the proprietors of that special morality of personal, caring relationships associated with the private sphere of the home. At the time in American history when the concept of the welfare state was beginning to be formulated, the entry of women into the political system as voters held special power for catalyzing the processes that began to "make the personal political."

In the midst of these conflicting interpretations, we return to our earlier assertion: We must remember that the most fundamental fact of the woman suffrage issue was its legislative formulation. As important as it is to understand suffrage in terms of lobbying activities, leadership activities, and social movement activities, the ultimate goal was to get laws passed at the state and national level enfranchising women. That it took great efforts to get the woman suffrage issue on the legislative agenda has been established by much historical scholarship. However, our question here is: What happened at that point when the woman suffrage issue was voted on in the national Congress?

For example, how did the actual voting patterns on woman suffrage link up with voting patterns on other legislation relevant to the interpretations summarized above? Can examination of legislative voting patterns on woman suffrage illuminate sources of support and of opposition to it and help resolve conflicting assessments of its connection to other issues in the Progressive Era? By looking at such legislative voting patterns, we hope to add a clarifying dimension to our understanding of feminism in the Progressive Era and the very heritage upon which is based the feminism of our own contemporary time period. With these perspectives in mind, we turn to an analysis of voting patterns on woman suffrage legislation in relation to civil rights, civil liberties, and social welfare legislation as voted upon by members of the House of Representatives.

DATA DEFINITION

Woman suffrage legislation was first voted on in the House of Representatives in 1915 in the 63rd Congress, where it was soundly defeated by a margin of 204 against to 174 in favor. In the 65th Congress in 1918, it was voted on again, where it passed in the House but was defeated in the Senate. Finally, in the 66th Congress in 1919, the woman suffrage amendment easily passed in the House by a margin of 304 in favor to 90 against, squeaked by a two-thirds majority in the Senate, and survived a cliff-hanging ratification process to become the Nineteenth Amendment to the Constitution on August 26, 1920.

To examine woman suffrage in relation to issues relevant to its interpretation as a "negative civil rights" issue or "social welfare" issue, we will look at roll call voting patterns in the 63rd, 65th, and 66th Congresses. All floor votes on woman suffrage, prohibition, black civil rights, child labor, and general labor issues will be considered. (See the Appendix for a list of all bills involved in floor votes analyzed in each of the selected Congresses.) Paired yeas and paired nays are added to the number of yeas and nays respectively cast; those absent or not voting are omitted from analysis. All votes on relevant issues are included if the division supporting and opposing the legislation is at least an 85%-15% split.

Status consistency connections with the woman suffrage issue will be examined by paying particularly close attention to how voting on the Nineteenth Amendment correlated with voting on Prohibition, immigration restriction, and black civil rights issues. The status consistency thesis suggests that the rural, Protestant, nativist American interests would package support for woman suffrage together with support for prohibition, immigration restriction, and restriction of black civil rights. However, if woman suffrage remains connected to civil rights concerns, we should find evidence to the contrary in the associations between these issues areas.

ANALYSIS: CIVIL RIGHTS AND SOCIAL WELFARE ISSUES CONNECTIONS

Our first question concerns the connection between woman suffrage and status consistency and civil rights issues. According to the Kraditor thesis, we should find woman suffrage positively associated with support for prohibition and support for immigration restriction. In addition, since we argue that status consistency issues involve civil rights and civil liberties principles, we might expect woman suffrage to be related negatively to such legislation as support for black civil rights.

Table 1 presents a striking picture bringing into serious question the validity of the Kraditor thesis in the context of the actual voting patterns of House members empowered to decide these legislative issues. One of the first surprises is the extremely low degree of association between woman suffrage and prohibition (average phi = | 0.163 |). Though these two issues have long been connected in historical accounts, it does not appear that House members voting

Table 1

Status Consistency Issue Area Connections,
House of Representatives, 63rd Congress, 1913-15

STATUS CONSISTENCY ISSUES

	Proh1	Proh2	Immig1	Immig3	Immig3	Immig4 (Race)	Race1	Race2	Race3
Suff1[a]	.267[b] ***	-.158 **	-.020	.060	.005	-.447 ***	-.144 **	-.384 **	.255 ***
Suff2	-.140 **	.088 *	.047	-.009	-.075	.467 ***	.359 ***	.616 ***	.486 ***
Proh1			.543 ***	.536 ***	-.527 ***	.128 **	.030	.018	-.032
Proh2			-.451 ***	-.472 ***	.452 ***	-.163 **	-.051	-.056	.089
Immig1						.240 ***	.175 **	.245 **	-.253 ***
Immig2						.185 ***	.084	.185 **	-.153 **
Immig3						-.269 ***	-.167 **	-.277 ***	.253 ***
Immig4 (Race)							.320 ***	.489 **	-.404 ***

[a]See Appendix A for citation of votes used in this analysis.
[b]Degree of association is Phi.
** p = .05, *** p = .001

for woman suffrage were in any way necessarily the same House members who were voting for prohibition. This finding suggests the importance of examining voting patterns in the institutional context of the national Congress as a source not only for verifying historical interpretations but perhaps for modifying them as well.

We also note with interest in Table 1 the lack of consistency among the immigration votes. The first three immigration votes are positively associated with prohibition, but the fourth immigration vote clearly stands apart. This is the proposal to restrict all immigration of blacks and of those of African descent. As indicated above, this categorical racial discrimination, in the face of no economic threat to labor interests, can be evaluated as a civil rights issue rather than an immigration issue per se. Indeed, Table 1 supports such an interpretation. The fourth immigration vote is positively associated with the three votes on black civil rights (involving the right of interracial marriage in the District of Columbia). Furthermore, we see that this fourth immigration vote (IMMIG 4) and black civil rights legislation (RACE 1, RACE 2, RACE 3) are all positively associated with woman suffrage. Most importantly, however, this association is not in the direction predicted by the Kraditor thesis: Those who voted for woman suffrage consistently voted against racist exclusionary immigration legislation (average phi = | .457 |).

When we expand this analysis to look at black civil rights issues per se, we find additional supporting evidence: Those who vote for woman suffrage also vote against the effort to outlaw interracial marriage in the District of Columbia (average phi = | .374 |). What is more, there is no statistically significant relationship between support for immigration restriction and the woman suffrage issue. Those in favor of or against immigration restriction did not have a characteristic position on woman suffrage. Thus, there is no evidence in Table 1 that rhetorical appeals to enfranchise women in order to stave off the inundation of uneducated immigrant voters, much less to ensure white supremacy, had any impact on the voting decisions of House members. Support for woman suffrage appears to have emanated from a source other than status consistency concerns.

We noted above that the first three immigration votes were positively associated with prohibition (average phi = | 0.500 |). It seems apparent that those who were seeking to control the number and type of immigrants to this country also were those who were more inclined to vote to outlaw all drinking for all inhabitants. This is very much as we would expect, and by comparison it throws into even greater relief the detachment of woman suffrage and other civil rights issues from prohibition and immigration legislation.

The analysis above calls into question the validity of linking the woman suffrage issue with other status consistency issues, and especially with racist orientations. Instead, we see support for considering the woman suffrage issue in terms of social justice concerns that also are reflected in black civil rights voting orientations. Prohibition, on the other hand, is highly associated with voting on immigration restrictions based on characteristics such as literacy (average phi = | .497 |), but is not strongly associated with the one immigration issue excluding all blacks (average phi = | .146 |), nor with voting on black civil rights. Thus, not only are prohibition and woman suffrage patterns unrelated to each other, they are differentially linked to immigration and black civil rights issues.

The voting patterns among issue areas presented in Table 1 argue strongly for the following reconceptualization of Progressive Era status consistency issue linkages: (1) Prohibition and suffrage are not highly associated; (2) the vote on the amendment to exclude all black immigrants is more correctly viewed as a black civil rights issue rather than an immigration issue; (3) prohibition voting is highly associated with immigration voting, defined in terms of restrictions based on such characteristics as literacy, but is unrelated to voting on immigration explicitly involving black civil rights issues; and (4) voting on woman suffrage is unrelated to voting on immigration regulation but is strongly associated with voting on immigration legislation involving black civil rights as well as legislation directly concerned with black civil rights issues.

To test these issue connections further, Table 2 reports the results of Guttman scaling analysis (with Goodenough-Edwards correction). From Table 2 it is clear that status consistency issues cannot be accurately viewed as aligning along a single dimension, since suffrage, prohibition, immigration, and black civil rights simply do not scale as a unit. (The coefficient of reproducibility of .740 is far

Table 2

Scalability of Status Consistency Issues (Guttman Scales), House of Representatives, 63rd Congress, 1913-15

*Guttman Scales**	Coefficient of Reproducibility	Coefficient of Scaleability
1. All Status Consistency Issue Votes:[a]	.740[b]	-.445[c]
Suff1 Suff2 Proh1 Proh2 Immig1 Immig2 Immig3 Immig4 (Race) Race1 Race2 Race3		
2. All Immigration and Race Votes:	.828	-.566
Immig1 Immig2 Immig3 Immig4 (Race)		
3. Immigration Votes Only:	.987	.954
Immig1 Immig2 Immig3		
4. Race Votes Only:	.992	.969
Race1 Race2 Race3 Immig4 (Race)		

*Goodenough-Edwards correction.
[a]See Appendix A for identification of roll call votes.
[b]Coefficient of Reproducibility should be .90 or above.
[c]Coefficient of Scaleability should be .60 or above.

below the necessary level of .90, and the coefficient of scalability is −.445, in no way approaching the necessary standard of .60 or above.)

In addition, Table 2 also demonstrates that the immigration and black civil rights issues do not line up on a single scalable dimension. When these issues are put on the same scale, both the coefficient of reproducibility and the coefficient of scalability are below necessary cutoffs for acceptable evidence of scalability. However, votes on immigration concerned with literacy requirements do form a separate scalable dimension, as do black civil rights votes on miscegenation taken together with categorical exclusion of all black immigrants. This latter scale has extremely high coefficients of reproducibility and scalability (.992 and .969 respectively), thereby adding important evidence that we are correct in viewing immigration legislation not as a single package, but as incorporating at least two dimensions. One of the more important findings is that the racist dimension based on principles of categorical exclusion of "racial nationalities" in fact does not scale with other immigration votes, but does scale with votes on black civil rights issues.

When we turn to the issue connections between woman suffrage and social welfare legislation, we see the somewhat complicated patterns that we would expect. Table 3 points to the fact that the strongest relationship is between support for woman suffrage and support for child labor restrictions. Clearly, at least to some degree there is an operating connection between women's "maternal sensibility" and the public sphere, specifically in relation to the welfare of children.

When it comes to the welfare of laborers, we see that there is a positive and statistically significant relationship between support for woman suffrage and for the social welfare of laborers. However, the degree of association is not as strong, and it is not difficult to understand why that is the case. American labor interests most often were ambivalent, if not hostile, to the woman suffrage issue. Not only were women typically viewed by labor union leaders as competitors to male labor interests, but woman suffrage was popularly associated with support for prohibition (as discussed above), a policy American labor vehemently opposed. These twin considerations produced a very problematic alliance between woman suffrage and labor legislation.

The woman suffrage amendment was voted on again in the House of Representatives in the 65th Congress, where it received a majority vote but not the necessary two-thirds majority vote for passage of a constitutional amendment. Finally, in the 66th Con-

Table 3

Civil Rights, Civil Liberties, and Social Welfare Issue Connections, House of Representatives, 63rd Congress, 1913-15

	SOCIAL WELFARE LEGISLATION					
	CHILD LABOR			LABOR		
Issue Votes[a]	ChLab1	ChLab2	ChLab3	Labor1	Labor2	Labor3
Suff1	.366[b] ***	-.323 ***	.373 ***	-.095 *	-.211 **	.327 ***
Suff2	-.317 ***	.396 ***	-.346 ***	.283 ***	.426 ***	-.432 ***
Proh1	-.083	.061	-.198 **	.026	-.069	.093
Immig1	-.244 ***	.180 **	-.199 **	.139 **	.105 *	-.011
Immig2	-.206 ***	.139 **	-.210 ***	.106 *	.013	.014
Immig3	.257 ***	-.189 **	.217 ***	-.140 ***	-.101 *	-.025
Immig4 (Race)	-.451 ***	.406 ***	-.562 ***	.234 ***	.289 ***	-.339 ***
Race1	-.163 **	.244 ***	-.181 **	.384 ***	.551 ***	-.288 ***
Race2	-.278 ***	.352 ***	-.289 ***	.485 ***	.635 ***	-.557 ***
Race3	.229 ***	-.311 ***	.222 ***	.516 ***	-.682 ***	.476 ***

[a]See Appendix A for votes used in analysis.
[b]Degree of association is Phi.
* p = .10, ** p = .05, *** p = .01

gress, the House of Representatives passed the woman suffrage amendment with a strong 77% majority victory.

From the perspective of this analysis, what is most interesting is that, although the percentage supporting woman suffrage increased dramatically in the House from 1915 to 1919, this shift was not accompanied by corresponding changes in issues connections. As Table 4 indicates, throughout the 63rd, 65th, and 66th Congresses, woman suffrage remained unconnected to such status consistency issues as immigration restriction, in contrast to prohibition, which retains its association with immigration restriction.

Further, as Table 5 demonstrates, in the 66th Congress woman suffrage and prohibition voting patterns remained unconnected in the House of Representatives, where both of these issues were passed as constitutional amendments.

As a final test of issue connections, Table 6 presents a factor analysis of the 1919 vote. Military issues have been included as a measure of the possible association between American involvement in World War I and the woman suffrage issue. We see in Table 6 confirmation that the patterns of issue connections exhibited in 1915 remained much the same through the 1915-1919 time period. Factor analysis does not reveal any single reform dimension linking all issues. Rather, as the rotated factor solution demonstrates in Table 6, prohibition is the dominant first factor, followed by suffrage combined on the second factor with labor and military issues, the third factor is immigration, and the fourth factor prohibition (civil rights) issues, accounting for a total variance of 71.3%. The highest correlation is between the prohibition factor (factor 1) and the immigration factor (factor 3), while there is virtually no correlation between the suffrage factor and the prohibition factor (factor 2 and factor 1 respectively) or between the suffrage factor and the immigration factor (factor 2 and factor 3 respectively). There is some correlation (though not very high) between the suffrage factor (factor 2) and the prohibition (civil rights) factor (factor 4), again indicating the linking of suffrage to due process concerns.

CONCLUSION

One of the most important findings illuminated by this analysis is the very great difference between the issue configurations found to be attached to woman suffrage and what would have been expected based on most historical accounts (Grimes 1967; Paulson 1973). We find that suffrage does not connect with status consistency issues designed to exert social control—if not restriction of civil rights and civil liberties—in the American political system. Rather,

Table 4

Patterns of Support between Issues Areas, 1913-1920,
House of Representatives, 63rd, 65th, 66th Congress

	SUFFRAGE AMENDMENT			PROHIBITION AMENDMENT		
Issue Votes	63rd Congress	65th Congress	66th Congress	63rd Congress	65th Congress	66th Congress
Immigration	not sig	not sig	not sig	.543 ***	.109 **	.107 *
Labor	.095[a] *	not sig	.417 ***	not sig	not sig	not sig
Child Labor	.327 ***	no votes	no votes	not sig	no votes	no votes
Woman Labor	.194 ***	no votes	no votes	no votes	no votes	not sig
Black Civil Rights, Immigration	-.144 **	no votes	no votes	not sig	no votes	no votes
Black Civil Rights, Race3	.255 ***	no votes	no votes	not sig	no votes	no votes
Black Civil Rights, Race2	-.447 ***	no votes	no votes	.128 *	no votes	no votes

[a]Degree of association is Phi; average Phi for immigration, labor, child labor and woman labor votes.
* p = .10, ** p = .05, *** p = .001

Table 5

Issue Connections, House of Representatives, 66th Congress, 1917-19

	Suff1	Proh1	Lab1	WomLab1	Immig1	Immig2	Immig3	Immig4	Proh5 CivRt1	Proh6 CivRt2
Suff1	--	.063[a]	.417 ***	.194 **	-.032	.267 ***	-.054	-.053	.134 **	-.287 ***
Proh1		--	-.079	.032	.107 *	-.315 ***	.593 ***	.598 ***	.301 ***	-.463 ***
Lab1			--	.266 ***	-.044	.174 **	-.044	-.091	.046	-.165 **
WomLab1				--	0	.074	.001	.044	.109	-.086
Immig1					--	-.060	.158 **	.179	.033	-.054
Immig2						--	-.392 ***	-.359 ***	-.216 ***	.148 **
Immig3							--	.869 ***	.199 ***	-.303 ***
Immig4								--	.205 ***	-.308 ***
CivRt1 Proh5										
CivRt2 Proh6										

[a]Degree of association is Phi.
* p = .10, ** p = .05, *** p = .01

woman suffrage was unconnected to immigration and prohibition legislation and was positively associated with support for black civil rights. This is immensely important to the debate over the "rights and justice" versus "expediency and utility" arguments that characterize suffrage analysis.

In addition, this research leads us to an important recognition: We must begin to differentiate between woman suffrage as a social movement and as a legislative issue. As a social movement, much was said and done on behalf of the suffrage cause, and it remains a problematic debate to distinguish between what suffrage leaders re-

Table 6

Rotated-Pattern Matrix for Woman Suffrage Issue Voting[a], *House of Representatives, 66th Congress, 1919-21*

Issue Votes	Prohibition	Suffrage Military Labor	Immigration	Civil Rights (Prohibition)
Proh1	.956	.014	.608	.277
Proh9	.954	.004	.607	.359
Proh11	.948	.028	.609	.239
Proh2	.927	-.006	.538	.345
Proh3	.926	.030	.538	.244
Proh15	-.926	-.027	-.627	-.301
Proh10	-.911	-.055	-.566	-.382
Proh8	-.898	-.012	-.493	-.470
Proh (Milt 5)	-.737	.113	-.410	-.330
Proh7	.725	.170	.344	.624
Proh4	-.529	-.186	-.327	-.437
Milt6	.105	.943	.120	.219
Milt2	.087	.927	.060	.128
Milt1	.005	.925	-.079	.192
Milt4	-.149	.683	-.199	.339
Labor1	-.048	.462	-.145	.335
Suff1	.098	.453	-.137	.441
Immig3	.594	.010	.925	.109
Immig4	.572	-.001	.914	.144
Proh6	-.544	-.204	-.272	-.766
Proh5	.337	.080	.192	.529
Percentage of Total Variance	46.0	17.2	5.6	3.5
Eigenvalue	9.67	3.61	1.18	.73

[a]An oblique rotation was chosen (oblimin) since correlations were evident between some issue areas. The pattern matrix is presented here which represents standardized regression weights of factors on each variable. The structure matrix is not reported here (representing correlations between each variable and each factor), since the clusterings are the same as for the pattern matrix. Initial extraction was principle axis factoring (PAF).

ally thought about immigration and racial issues and what they were willing to say in order to win support in the battle to get legislation enacted. Though this in no way excuses what is basically unpardonable racist rhetoric in the suffrage legacy, it nevertheless raises the question whether such sentiments were the result of deeply felt biases or were pragmatic tolls viewed as necessary to pay the price of enfranchisement.

However, when we switch to woman suffrage as a legislative issue, it is not so much the rhetoric of lobbying as the decision-making process itself that becomes the focus of attention. The long-neglected arena of legislative activity is where we can determine not only the partisan, regional, and constituency influences related to suffrage support but also the characteristic alignments between woman suffrage and the civil rights and social welfare legislation also considered throughout the same time period.

When we look at the legislators who voted on suffrage—rather than the activists who lobbied for suffrage—and the relations to voting positions on other issues, we find a pattern of issues connections very different from what has been identified heretofore. We do not find support for connecting suffrage to a status consistency package; rather, we find evidence that suffrage was associated until the very end with issues of rights and justice.

Another consequence of our analysis is the recognition that status consistency issues do not merely involve a principle of social control common to all forms of regulation. Rather, we contend that status consistency issues need to be reconceptualized in civil rights terms. It is not merely that prohibition proponents attempted to preserve a rural, Protestant, nativist American life-style, but rather that the formula for this preservation was legal and absolute deprivation of the rights and liberties of any and all individuals to make basic personal life-style decisions involving alcoholic beverages. Social control, in the case of prohibition, was not a regulative or educationally oriented piece of legislation, as temperance had been decades before. Rather, prohibition was a negative civil rights issue elevated to the level of a Constitutional amendment.

Not only is it significant that the woman suffrage issue was not related to prohibition support and not related to the restriction of black civil rights, but we can newly appreciate woman suffrage in another way as a consequence of this analysis. That is, woman suffrage becomes the one and only positive civil rights issue considered by the 63rd, 64th, 65th, and 66th Congresses. Other civil rights issues—prohibition, a ban on interracial marriage in the District of Columbia, and a total ban on all black and African immigration—are civil rights issues, as we have argued, but they are civil rights issues proposed in the negative format of depriving, rather than extending, basic rights to individuals. The woman suffrage issue takes on new significance in the context of civil rights concerns. Not only is it positively connected to support for other civil rights issues voted on in the same period, but it is the single positive formulation of civil rights considered in this phase of the Progressive Era.

Thus, a new look at the Nineteenth Amendment discloses its significance both for the Progressive Era and for contemporary politics. Woman suffrage was the only positive civil rights issue considered in the 63rd to 66th Congresses. Attention to this dimension invites us to reformulate "status consistency" issues in terms of the civil rights and civil liberties principles they involve. Also, analysis of the dynamics accounting for the shift in support for suffrage in the House from 1915 to 1919 in the context of a nonrealignment period reveals the importance of state-level constituencies, suggesting a fruitful investigative approach to apply to other legislative issues in the Progressive Era (McDonagh, 1990).

We have argued that the significance of the Nineteenth Amendment that initiated women as full political citizens is felt today at the level of grass-roots politics, at the level of elite political leadership, and even at the level of political culture itself. Women are voting at (often) higher rates than men and with more clearly identified partisan orientations. Women are participating as political candidates and as managers of key presidential campaigns. Finally, the American political culture reflects the heritage of both the feminist reform period of 1900 to 1920 and the feminist reform period of 1960 to 1970, which declared that the personal is, and must be, political.

Thus we can appreciate, participate in, and analyze contemporary gender gap politics, all the while noting the significance of the Nineteenth Amendment upon which it all rests.

NOTES

1. Nancy Cott (1985) accounts for this neglect on the following grounds. First, woman suffrage was virtually the only "visible" women's issue included—though superficially and briefly to be sure—in standard texts in American history prior to the women's movement in academia, at a time when the scholarly mission was partly defined as finding the "invisible" women who constituted historical and political reality. Second, woman suffrage was viewed as an upper-middle-class, "elite" social movement at odds with the initial concerns among women's studies scholars to reacknowledge and revalue the lives and contributions of women who were less privileged from a social-class and economic perspective. Third, woman suffrage was discounted as simply a legal, formal achievement that left unaffected major structural arrangements that remained to the disadvantage of women in basic societal institutions such as the family and the paid labor force. Fourth, the political payoff for women upon their enfranchisement did not seem to materialize, either in the form of turnout at elections or in the form of interest group activity articulating issue concerns of particular importance to women.

2. For analyses questioning the nature of the connection between woman suffrage and prohibition, see Blocker (1985), Bordin (1981), and McDonagh and Price (1985).

3. Thanks to Aage Clausen for first confirming (in conversation with the author) the possibility of classifying prohibition as a civil rights, civil liberties issue.

REFERENCES

Blocker, Jack S. 1985. "Separate Paths: Suffragists and the Women's Temperance Crusade." *Signs* 10(3): 460-476.

Bordin, Ruth. 1981. *Women and Temperance: The Quest for Power and Liberty, 1873-1900*. Philadelphia: Temple University Press.

Buhle, Mari Jo, and Paul Buhle, eds. 1978. *The Concise History of Woman Suffrage: Selections From the Classic Work of Stanton, Anthony, Gage, and Harper*. Urbana, IL: University of Illinois Press.

Cott, Nancy F. 1985. Keynote Address, Women's History Week, Harvard University, Cambridge, Massachusetts.

Cott, Nancy F. 1987. *The Grounding of Modern Feminism*. New Haven, CT: Yale University Press.

Filene, Peter G. 1970. "An Obituary for 'The Progressive Movement.'" *American Quarterly* 22: 20-34.

Grimes, Alan P. 1967. *The Puritan Ethic and Woman Suffrage*. New York: Oxford University Press.

Katzenstein, Mary Fainsod. 1984. "Feminism and the Meaning of the Vote." *Signs* 10(1): 4-26.

Kleppner, Paul. 1982. "Were Women to Blame? Female Suffrage and Voter Turnout," *Journal of Interdisciplinary History*, XII:4, 621-643.

Kraditor, Aileen S. 1965. *The Ideas of the Woman Suffrage Movement, 1880-1920*. New York: Columbia University Press.

McDonagh, Eileen L., and H. Douglas Price. 1985. "Woman Suffrage in the Progressive Era: Patterns of Opposition and Support in Referenda Voting, 1910-1918." *American Political Science Review* 79(2): 415-435.

McDonagh, Eileen. 1989. "Issues and Constituencies in the Progressive Era: House Roll Call Voting on the Nineteenth Amendment, 1913-1919."*Journal of Politics*, 51:1, 119-136.

Mueller, Carol M. 1988. "The Empowerment of Women: Polling and the Women's Voting Bloc." In *The Politics of the Gender Gap: The Social Construction of Political Influence*, ed. Carol Mueller. Newbury Park, CA: Sage Publications.

Ostrander, Susan A. October 1989. Feminism, Voluntarism, and the Welfare State: Moving Toward a Feminist Sociological Theory of Social Welfare. *The American Sociologist* (Spring): 29-41.

Paulson, Ross Evans. 1973. *Women's Suffrage and Prohibition*. Glenview, IL: Scott, Foresman and Co.

APPENDIX

House of Representatives Roll Call Votes

Variable numbers and descriptions of bills are from *Code Book*, ICPSR 0004, Interuniversity Consortium for Political and Social Research, University of Michigan; the variable label refers to labels used in the text. "Yes" and "no" votes in parentheses include paired yeas and paired nays.

<u>House of Representatives, 63rd Congress</u>

SUFF 1	H.J. Res 1 (v248)	Propose to the state legislatures a woman's suffrage amendment to the Constitution. (yes = 186, no = 210)
SUFF 2	H.J. Res 1 (v247)	To order the previous question on striking out

		the enacting clause from H.J. Res 1 which would defeat this resolution to amend the Constitution and grant woman suffrage. (yes = 207, no = 169)
PROH 1	H.J. Res 168 (v238)	On passage of H.J. 168, Res submitting a prohibition amendment to the state legislatures for ratification. (yea = 197, nay = 211)
PROH 2	H.J. Res 168 (v237)	To amend H.J. Res requiring the admission of a prohibition resolution to state conventions, rather than to state legislatures, as provided in the resolution. (yes = 176, no = 211)
CHLAB 1	H.R. 12292	To suspend the rules and

	(v269)	pass the Bill H.R. 12292, a bill preventing products of child-labor from being entered in interstate commerce. (yes = 237, no = 45)
CHLAB 2	H.R. 12292 (v265)	To adjourn, during debate on H.R. 12292. (yes = 63, no = 201)
CHLAB 3	H.R. 12292 (v266)	To order a second to a motion made to suspend the rules during consideration of the bill H.R. 12291. (yes = 213, no = 47)
LABOR 1	H.R. 15657 (Clayton Act) (v134)	To pass H.R. 15657, a bill to supplement existing laws against unlawful restraints and monopolies and for other purposes. (yes = 290, no = 66)
LABOR 2	H.R. 15657 (v209)	To pass conference report #1168 on H.R. 15657. (yes = 261, no = 66)

LABOR 3	H.R. 1933 (v103)	To amend H.R. 1933 to prohibit interstate transportation of convict labor made goods. (yes = 80, no = 218)
RACE 1	H.R. 1710 (v246)	To pass H.R. 1710, a bill prohibiting and punishing miscegenation in the District of Columbia and voiding such intermarriage. (yes = 239, no = 60)
RACE 2	H.R. 1710 (v244)	To order the previous question on passage of H.R. 1710. (yes = 175, no = 119)
RACE 3	H.R. 1710 (v245)	To recommit H.R. 1710. (yes = 90, no = 201)
IMMIG 4 (Race)	H.R. 6060 (v243)	To concur in Senate Amendment No. 18 to H.R. 6060, a bill regulating the immigration of aliens and their residence in the

		U.S.; which amendment would exclude all members of the African or black race from immigration into the U.S. (yes = 78, no = 257)
IMMIG 1	H.R. 6060 (v93)	To pass H.R. 6060, regulating immigration of aliens to and residence in the United States. (yes = 263, no = 138)
IMMIG 2	H.R. 6060 (v262)	On passage over the President's veto of the bill H.R. 6060. (yes = 269, no = 141)
IMMIG 3	H.R. 6060 (v92)	To recommit H.R. 6060 to the Committee on Immigration and Naturalization with instructions to eliminate literacy requirement. (yes = 150, no = 249)
MILT 1	H.R. 14034	To amend the amendment of

	(v148)	Mr. Padgett to H.R. 14034, a bill making appropriations for the naval service for fiscal 1915, by eliminating provision for building a new battleship. (yes = 106, no = 154)
MILT 2	H.R. 14034 (v149)	To concur in Senate Amendment #71 to H.R. 14034. (yes = 176, no = 90)
MILT 3	H.R. 20975 (v263)	To recommit the naval appropriation bill so it will be amended to authorize construction of one battleship instead of two. (yes = 155, no = 172)
MILT 6	H.R. 21491 (v278)	Committee of the Whole to consider war fortifications bill. (yes = 182, no = 103)
MILT 7	S. 6357 (v195)	To pass war risk insurance. (yes = 233, no = 62)

House of Representatives, 66th Congress

SUFF 1	H.J. Res 1 (v12)	To pass H.J. Res 1 proposing an amendment to the Constitution extending the right of suffrage to women. (yes = 309, no = 91)
PROH 1	H.R. 6810 (v53)	To pass H.R. 6810, a bill to prohibit intoxicating beverages. (yes = 295, no = 105)
PROH 2	H.R. 6810 (v122)	To pass H.R. 6810 over the President's veto. (yes = 210, no = 73)
PROH 3	H.R. 161 (v36)	To pass H.R. 161, authorizing the House to resolve itself into the Committee of the Whole and take up H.R. 6810. (yes = 233, no = 62)
PROH 4	H.R. 6810 (v48)	To adjourn, a motion made during consideration of H.R. 6810. (yes = 150, no = 219)

PROH 5	H.R. 6810 (v49)	To amend H.R. 6810, by empowering state officers to issue search warrants. (yes = 73, no = 286)
PROH 6	H.R. 6810 (v50)	To amend H.R. 6810, waiving requirement of a bond from five hundred to five thousand dollars. (yes = 218, no = 153)
PROH 7	H.R. 6810 (v51)	To amend H.R. 6810, by authorizing the issuance of search warrants against private dwellings, where liquor is illegally sold. (yes 211, no = 166)
PROH 8	H.R. 6810 (v52)	To recommit H.R. 6810 to the Committee on the Judiciary. (yes = 141, no = 262)
PROH 9	H.R. Res 331 (v107)	To pass H.R. Res 331, providing immediately upon

		adoption of this resolution, House proceed to consideration of report on H.R. 6810. (yes = 219, no = 89)
PROH 10	H.R. 6810 (v108)	Recommit conference report on H.R. 6810, insisting upon disagreement to issue search warrants. (yes = 83, no = 218)
PROH 11	H.R. 6810 (v109)	Adopt conference report on H.R. 6810. (yes = 230, no = 69)
PROH 12	H.R. 12610 (v183)	To recommit H.R. 12610 with instructions to report back with amendment, repealing prohibition as of July 1st, 1920. (yes = 95, no = 265)
LABOR 1	H.R. 4438 (v114)	To pass H.R. 4438, a bill to provide for the promotion of vocational rehabilitation of persons disabled in

		industry or otherwise and their return to civil employment. (yes = 207, no = 116)
IMMIG 1	H.R. 14461 (v260)	A bill providing for suspension of immigration into the U.S. (yes = 316, no = 60)
IMMIG 2	H.R. 14461 (v326)	To agree to the conference report on H.R. 14461. (yes = 301, no = 45)
MILT 1	H.J. Res 327 (v233)	To concur in the Senate amendment to H.J. Res 327, relating to the ratification of the peace treaty with Germany. (yes = 237, no = 148)
MILT 2	S. 120 (v25)	Table Mr. Moon's appeal from the Chair's decision, made during debate on S. 120, repealing joint resolution authorizing President during

		time of war to take over control of the communications systems. (yes = 188, no = 161)
MILT 3	S. 2236 (v84)	To pass S. 2236, a bill extending protection to civil rights of members of the military. (yes = 182, no = 63)
MILT 4	(v261)	To suspend war laws. (yes = 94, no = 206)
MILT 5	H.J. Res 382 (v341)	To order previous question on H.J. Res 382 declaring certain acts of Congress, shall be construed as if the war had ended. (yes = 185, no = 131)

Justice Sandra Day O'Connor and the Supreme Court's Reaction to Its First Female Member

Karen O'Connor
Jeffrey A. Segal

SUMMARY. On July 7, 1981, President Ronald Reagan fulfilled one of his campaign promises: He appointed Judge Sandra Day O'Connor of the Arizona Court of Appeals to be the first female Justice to serve on the U.S. Supreme Court. Most early commentators agreed that Judge O'Connor fit the conservative mold of other Reagan appointees. Nevertheless, women's groups universally hailed her appointment as a major breakthrough for women in general and for the advancement of women's rights through the courts in particular. The simple purpose of this modest paper, which is part of a larger study, is to address the question of whether those expectations were correct. More specifically, we examine all 55 sex discrimination cases decided by the Burger Court—both before and after the appointment of Justice O'Connor—to determine her impact on the Court as a whole and upon individual Justices.

METHODOLOGY AND EXPECTATIONS

The 55 cases selected for analysis include all cases decided by the Burger Court based on the Fourteenth or Fifteenth Amendment to the U.S. Constitution, Title VII or Title IX of the Civil Rights and Education Amendments respectively, or the Equal Pay Act in which a state, federal, or private action was challenged as sexually discriminatory. Voting patterns of the Justices are identified by the use of cumulative scaling of all nonunanimous decisions. We then use

---

Karen O'Connor is affiliated with Emory University. Jeffrey A. Segal is affiliated with the State University of New York at Stony Brook.

simple crosstabulation in a preliminary effort to assess the effect of the addition of Justice O'Connor to the bench.

Little research has been done by scholars of the judicial process to determine the effect of a single Justice on the Court. In particular, no studies exist concerning the possible impact that the appointment of Justice Marshall had on the other Justices in terms of their sensitivity to the issue of race discrimination. His appointment, however, occurred during the so-called heyday of the Court's liberal approach to race discrimination claims, and it is unlikely that any immediately discernable impact took place. In contrast, Justice O'Connor was appointed to a Court which, while generally supportive of sex discrimination complaints (O'Connor and Epstein 1983), had yet to apply the strict scrutiny standard used to resolve racial complaints to claims involving gender bias.

Studies by Gryski and Dixon (1986) and by Gryski and Main (1986) suggest that the presence of a woman on a collegial court increases the likelihood that the court will decide in favor of a sex discrimination claim. Their findings on this point are quite tentative; nonetheless, there could be many reasons for this phenomenon. The presence of a woman on the bench, particularly on one long comprised solely of men, may serve to sensitize the Justices to issues of sex discrimination. Conversely, the Justices may want to show their newest member that they are not sexist and may therefore bend over backward to support claims of sex discrimination. Thus we hypothesize:

1. The Court as a whole will become more supportive of sex discrimination complaints after the addition of Justice O'Connor.

Traditionalists (Abraham 1982; Funston 1977; Wasby 1976) and behavioralists (Carp and Rowland 1983; Goldman 1983; Segal 1985) long have noted the effects of additions to the Court. One aspect of personnel change involves the so-called "freshman effect" (Heck 1979; Heck and Hall 1981; Scheb and Ailshie 1985). Heck and Hall, for example, observe that, with the notable exception of Justice Stevens, new Justices tend to vote with ideological blocs. Other scholars have concluded that Justice O'Connor has aligned herself with the conservative bloc on the Court (Scheb and Ailshie 1985, 11). Thus we hypothesize:

2. Justice O'Connor will vote with the conservative bloc of the Court in sex discrimination cases.

FINDINGS

O'Connor and Epstein (1983) found that the U.S. Supreme Court supported sex discrimination claims in 58.8% of the 68 cases they examined for the 1969 to 1981 terms. As revealed in Table 1, the Burger Court adopted a pro-equality position in 63% of the cases it decided. Additionally, as revealed in Table 1, four Justices routinely evidenced support for the pro-equality position substantially above the Court mean—Brennan (90%), Marshall (83%), O'Connor (75%), and White (74%). Justices Stevens and Blackmun emerged as the centrist members of the Court, while Justices Burger, Rehnquist, and Powell were the most consistently negative with regard to sex discrimination claims.

An examination of the Court's support for sex discrimination claims *after* the appointment of Justice O'Connor, however, reveals a slightly different pattern. In fact, an overall rise in the Court's support for these cases occurred—75% vs. 63%—a finding consistent with Hypothesis 1. Indeed, Justices O'Connor and Blackmun are the "swing" Justices on this Court.

The importance of these two Justices' votes can be seen in Table 2, which contains a cumulative scaling of the nonunanimous decisions of the Court rendered after the appointment of Justice Stevens. The cases fit well-recognized standards of scalability (Rohde and Spaeth 1976). The coefficient of reproducibility (CR) is .92, well above the .90 threshold, while the coefficient of scalability (S) is .7522, above the .60 guideline.

When we focus our attention on the individual Justices' support for sex discrimination complaints after Justice O'Connor's appointment, several interesting changes can be observed. As revealed in Table 3, the rank order and degree of support changed markedly. In general, while the support of Justice Brennan—the Justice whom Brenner and Spaeth (1986) found to be the sole issue specialist on

TABLE 1. Burger Court Support for Sex Discrimination Claims

JUSTICE	SUPPORT (%)	N of CASES
Court	63.0	54
Brennan	90.4	52
Marshall	83.3	54
O'Connor	75.0	12
White	74.1	54
Stevens	64.1	39
Blackmun	54.0	50
Stewart	48.8	41
Powell	41.2	51
Burger	32.7	52
Rehnquist	25.5	51

gender discrimination – dipped a bit (83.3% vs. 92.7%), and that of Justice Powell stayed about the same (41.7% vs. 42.5%), all of the other Justices' support for these claims increased when Justice O'Connor was added to the Court. Justice White's support increased by more than 20% (91.7% vs. 69.8%), Justice Stevens rose from 57.1% to 83.3%, and even Chief Justice Burger's support rose considerably (32.1% to 50%). Even more remarkable was the increase in Justice Rehnquist's support: His support actually doubled!

The reasons for these changes may go beyond the addition of Justice O'Connor. Cases, however, did not get easier during this period (Maltz, 1985). Thus it is clear that our findings support Hypothesis 1: The Court clearly became more receptive to sex discrimination claims after the appointment of Justice O'Connor.

TABLE 2. Cumulative Scaling of Nonunanimous Sex Discrimination Cases

# of Cases	JUSTICES: Ma	Br	Wh	Stv	O'C	Bl	Stw	Po	Bu	Re	Total
2	+	+	+	+		+	+	+	+	−	8−1
1	+	+	+	+		+	+	+	−	−	7−2
1	+	+	+	+	+	+		−	+	−	7−2
1	+	+	+	+	+	−		−	+	+	7−2
1	+		+	+		+	+	+	−	−	6−2
1	+	+	+	+		+	+	−	−	−	6−3
1	+	+	+	+	+	+		−	−	−	6−3
1	+	+	−			+	+	−	−	+	5−3
3	+	+	+	+		+	−	−	−	−	5−4
1	+	+	+	+	+	−		−	−	−	5−4
2	+	+	+	+		−	−	+	−	−	5−4
1	+	+	+	−		+	−	−	−	−	4−5
1	+	+	−	+		−	+	−	−	−	4−5
1	+	+	+	+		−	−	−	−	−	4−5
1	+	+	+	+	−	−		−	−	−	4−5
1	+	+	−	+		−	−	−	−	−	3−6
1	+	−	+	−	−	+		−	−	−	3−6
2	+	+	+	−		−	−	−	−	−	3−6
1	−	+	−	−		−	+	−	−	+	3−6
1	−	−	+	−		+	−	+	−	−	3−6
2	+	+	−	−		−	−	−	−	−	2−7
	25−2	24−2	21−6	18−8	4−2	14−13	8−13	7−20	4−23	3−24	

\+ = pro-equality position   R = .92
− = anti-equality position   S = .752

TABLE 3. Rank Order of Justices' Support for Sex Discrimination Claims, Pre- and Post- O'Connor Appointment

Pre-O'Connor Appointment		Post-O'Connor Appointment	
Brennan	92.7%	Marshall	91.7%
Marshall	81.4%	White	91.7%
White	69.8%	Brennan	83.3%
Stevens	57.1%	Stevens	83.3%
Blackmun	50%	O'Connor	75%
Powell	42.5%	Blackmun	63.6%
Burger	32.1%	Burger	50%
Rehnquist	25%	Rehnquist	50%
n = 55		Powell	41.7%
		n = 12	

Our second hypothesis posited that Justice O'Connor's behavior would follow that of others who experienced the freshman effect—namely, that she would vote with the ideologically conservative bloc. As revealed in Tables 1, 2, and 3, this did *not* occur. Clearly, Justice O'Connor's voting behavior on sex discrimination claims makes her a "centrist" Justice (Segal 1986). Others, however (Cook 1986; Scheb and Ailshie 1985), have found that O'Connor indeed voted with the conservative bloc on most issues. Thus, in cases involving issues of sex discrimination, Justice O'Connor often parts company with her conservative allies. While she is not in the liberal vanguard, she clearly moves to the center when cases involving gender are decided by the Court. We must, therefore, reject our second hypothesis, while noting that the addition of Justice O'Connor did not install a Justice as favorably disposed to sex discrimination complaints as four of her Brethren. Feminist hopes clearly cannot be staked on Justice O'Connor, although the addition of Justices Scalia and Kennedy may force her further to the left in these kinds of cases.

CONCLUSION

In this paper, we found that the Court as a whole, and the majority of its individual members, became more supportive of sex discrimination complaints after Justice O'Connor's appointment to the High Court. In fact, prior to the appointment of Justice O'Connor to the Court, unanimous decisions concerning sex discrimination were rare; since her appointment, however, numerous cases involving a variety of different allegedly discriminatory practices or laws have been decided unanimously. Cases involving Title VII, the Social Security Act, sexual harassment, retirement benefits, and women's exclusion from private clubs have been decided in favor of the victims of sex discrimination.

This pattern leads directly to one of our most important findings, the dramatic rise in Chief Justice Rehnquist's support for sex discrimination complaints. While his overall support clearly lags behind the Court as a whole, he has supported the party charging sex discrimination 50% of the time. Given his prior record and his elevation to the position of Chief Justice, this change is likely to bode well for the future resolution of sex discrimination cases. As the Chief Justice, he is in the position to mold the Court to some extent. Clearly, he is not as conservative as some of his most vocal critics have charged—at least in terms of sex discrimination cases. Whether the change in his stance or in that of the rest of the Justices is due to the appointment of Justice O'Connor and directly attributable to her presence on the bench is impossible to determine with total accuracy. Nevertheless, a noticeable change occurred on the Court toward sex discrimination complaints when she took her place.

Another interesting finding revealed here is Justice Powell's low support for sex discrimination complaints. After the appointment of Justice O'Connor, Justice Powell's relatively low support for women's rights remained constant, leaving him as the least supportive Justice of women's rights claims. It is highly improbable that his replacement, Justice Kennedy, will be much more conservative. Thus it is unlikely that major shifts will soon be forthcoming.

We also found that, contrary to the predictions of feminists or of "freshman effect" scholars, Justice O'Connor turned out to be a key swing Justice on issues of sex discrimination. Moreover, with the recent additions of conservative Justices Scalia and Kennedy, her presence on the Court could take on greater importance. Clearly, as revealed in Table 2, her vote was pivotal in several cases. Most notably, in *Mississippi University for Women v. Hogan* (1982), Justice O'Connor, writing for the 5-4 majority, stressed her belief that the exclusion of men from state-supported nursing schools perpetuated sex role stereotypes and further depressed women's wages by keeping nursing a female-dominated profession. Prior to her appointment, the Court had split 4 to 4 in *Vorchheimer v. School District of Philadelphia* (1977), letting stand a lower court ruling allowing sex-segregated high schools. However, in *Ohio Civil Rights Commission v. Dayton Christian Schools, Inc.* (1986), another 5-4 decision, Justice O'Connor sided with the conservative bloc to cast the deciding vote in a pregnancy discrimination case. According to the narrow majority, the nonrenewal of a pregnant teacher's contract was justified by the school's religious doctrine, which held that women should stay at home with their children. In *Dayton*, when faced with competing First Amendment and equal protection views, the rights entitled to strict scrutiny (free exercise of religion) won out with Justice O'Connor over the lower, intermediate standard of review used in gender cases. When competing constitutional claims have not been present in other pregnancy cases, such as *Newport News Shipbuilding and Dry Dock Co. v. EEOC* (1983) and, more recently, *California Federal Savings and Loan Association v. Guerra* (1987), Justice O'Connor has voted against discrimination against pregnant workers.

The addition of the new Justices and the potential for the Court to swing further to the right leave Justice O'Connor in an especially important position. She now has the opportunity to take a more vocal role, should she so desire, to maintain the status quo or to set the Court on a more liberal path in this area of the law. Clearly, that choice will be hers and hers alone. Feminists can only hope that Justice O'Connor, as someone who has faced discrimination, will come to view her role as a spokesperson on the Court for an under-represented group and will join Justice Brennan as a liberal specialist when issues of gender discrimination are at stake.

REFERENCES

Abraham, Henry A. 1982. *Freedom and the Court*, 4th ed. New York: Oxford University Press.

Brenner, Saul, and Harold Spaeth. 1986. "Issue Specialization in Majority Opinion Assignment on the Burger Court." *Western Political Quarterly* 39:520-527.

California Federal Savings and Loan Association v. Guerra. 1987. 479 U.S. 272.

Carp, Robert A., and C. K. Rowland. 1983. *Policymaking and Politics and the Federal District Courts*. Knoxville: University of Tennessee Press.

Cook, Beverly. 1986. Justice Sandra Day O'Connor and the Uses of Federalism as a Decisional Principle. Prepared for delivery at the annual meeting of the American Political Science Association.

Funston, Richard. 1977. *Constitutional Counterrevolution*. New York: John Wiley.

Goldman, Sheldon. 1983. "Reagan Judicial Appointments at Midterm: Shaping the Bench in His Own Image." *Judicature* 66:334-347.

Gryski, Gerard, and William Dixon. 1986. "Models of State High Court Decision Making in Sex Discrimination Cases." *Journal of Politics* 48:143-155.

Gryski, Gerard, and Eleanor C. Main. 1986. "Social Backgrounds as Predictors of Votes on State Courts of Last Resort." *Western Political Quarterly* 39:528-537.

Heck, Edward V. 1979. "The Socialization of the Freshman Justice: The Early Years of Justice Brennan." *Pacific Law Journal* 10:707.

Heck, Edward V., and Melinda Gann Hall. 1981. "Black Voting and the Freshman Justice Revisited." *Journal of Politics* 43:852-860.

Maltz, Earl M. 1985. "Sex Discrimination in the Supreme Court." *Duke Law Journal* 1985:177-194.

Mississippi University for Women v. Hogan. 1982. 458 U.S. 718.

Newport News Shipbuilding and Dry Dock Co. v. EEOC 1983. 462 U.S. 669.

O'Connor, Karen, and Lee Epstein. 1983. "Sex and the Supreme Court: An Analysis of Support for Gender-Based Claims." *Social Science Quarterly* 64:327-331.

Ohio Civil Rights Commission v. Dayton Christian Schools, Inc. 1986. 477 U.S. 619.

Rohde, David, and Harold Spaeth. 1976. *Supreme Court Decision Making*. San Francisco: W. H. Freeman.

Scheb, John, and Lee Ailshie. 1985. "Justice Sandra Day O'Connor and the Freshman Effect." *Judicature* 69:9-12.

Segal, Jeffrey A. 1985. "Measuring Change on the Supreme Court: Examining Alternative Models." *American Journal of Political Science* 29:461-479.

Segal, Jeffrey A. 1986. "Supreme Court Justices as Human Decision Makers: An Individual-Level Analysis of Search and Seizure Cases." *Journal of Politics* 48:941-952.

Vorchheimer v. School District of Philadelphia. 1977. 430 U.S. 406.

Wasby, Stephen. 1976. *Continuity and Change From the Warren to Burger Court*. Pacific Palisades, CA: Goodyear.

When Should Differences Make a Difference: A New Approach to the Constitutionality of Gender-Based Laws

Susan Gluck Mezey

SUMMARY. This study criticizes the Supreme Court's current approach to constitutional gender equality and suggests a new type of review for gender-based classifications under the equal protection clause. The debate over acceptable gender classifications has forced the Court to decide whether distinctions on the basis of gender-specific physical characteristics discriminate on the basis of gender, whether legislation on the basis of generalized physical characteristics is discriminatory when applied to individuals who deviate from the average, whether states reinforce sex role stereotypes when legislating on the basis of gender-specific physical characteristics, and whether legislation that purports to benefit women actually serves to further inequality. In wrestling with these issues, especially the last, the Court has also been forced to explain both logically and legally why racial classifications are different from gender classifications.

The purpose of this study is twofold: The first objective is to argue that the Supreme Court should adopt an approach to legally sanctioned gender differentiation that would review gender classifications with the same hostility as racial classifications; related to this is the second objective, which is to show that a strict-scrutiny equal protection analysis is compatible with a special treatment approach for pregnancy benefits legislation. The two tasks will be undertaken by presenting critiques of the Court's current approach to gender equity and by suggesting an alternative direction for gender-based equal protection doctrine, one that will accommodate positive pregnancy legislation.

Susan Gluck Mezey is affiliated with Loyola University.

The equal protection clause of the Fourteenth Amendment puts states on notice that they must justify their decisions to treat individuals as legally different. Differential treatment is permissible when it is based upon *relevant* differences among the subjects of the classification; for almost 20 years, the Supreme Court has struggled to develop a constitutional doctrine to judge legislative assertions of relevant differences between men and women in light of the command of the equal protection clause.

In this article, *sex* is regarded as a biological characteristic and *gender* as a culturally and historically derived attribute.[1] "The fact that women bear children is due to sex; that women nurture children is due to gender, a cultural construct" (Lerner 1986, 21). I assert that legal gender classifications are never appropriate and that sex-based classifications must be limited to pregnancy legislation that has no adverse impact upon women. Toward this end, I argue that the Supreme Court should review legislative classifications pertaining to men and women with the same hostility as it does racial classifications and subject them, like race, to "scrutiny that [is] 'strict' in theory and fatal in fact" (Gunther 1972, 8; see also Kirp and Robyn 1979, 949). I also argue that preferential treatment of pregnancy can survive strict scrutiny by analogizing it to compensatory racial legislation.[2]

THE CURRENT APPROACH TO CONSTITUTIONAL GENDER-BASED CASES

From 1971, the onset of the Supreme Court's modern phase of gender decision-making, until the present, there have been 25 decisions on equal protection challenges to state and federal laws involving male-female distinctions; only a bare majority, 13, were struck down by the highest court.[3] Eighteen of these cases were brought by men, six were brought by women, and one was brought jointly by a husband and wife. As Table 1 shows, the Court upheld the gender classification in 10 of the 18 suits brought by men and in two of the six brought by women. In these cases the Court accepted the legislative classification for one of two reasons: compensation for past societal discrimination against women or physical differences between the sexes.[4]

In the compensation cases, the Court approved a widows-only property tax exemption (*Kahn v. Shevin* 1974), upheld a Navy regulation allowing women more time in rank than men to be promoted

(*Schlesinger v. Ballard* 1975), allowed women a more favorable method of computing earnings for Social Security benefits for a limited period of time (*Califano v. Webster* 1977), and sanctioned a five-year exception to a pension offset provision for women but not for men (*Heckler v. Mathews* 1984).[5]

These classifications were upheld because they satisfied the Court's requirement of sufficiently tailored remedies for past discrimination against women. According to Wendy Williams (1982), however, these decisions "perpetuate the very separate sphere stereotypes that the Court no longer tolerates as the basis for legislation that treats women *less* favorably than men" (180, n. 35, emphasis in the original). By refusing to apply strict scrutiny, the Court treated gender-based benign discrimination as analytically distinct from racial-based benign discrimination and, in the name of compensation, upheld questionable laws that could not have passed the more searching scrutiny of race cases (see also Baer 1983, and Ginsburg 1978).[6]

The second category consists of decisions prompted by challenges to regulations relating to physical differences between the sexes. Far from utilizing strict scrutiny, however, the Court went so far as to ignore its own less strict "heightened scrutiny" standard formally adopted in *Craig v. Boren* (1976) and required only that the legislation satisfy a test of reasonableness or rationality. This legislation typically survives judicial scrutiny, given the reality of physical differences between the sexes and the minimal demands of the rationality test.

In these cases, the Court upheld a sex-specific statutory rape law (*Michael M. v. Superior Court* 1981), allowed male-only military registration (*Rostker v. Goldberg* 1981), approved California's exclusion of pregnancy disability benefits (*Geduldig v. Aiello* 1974), and withheld benefits and rights in four cases of unwed fathers and illegitimate children (*Fiallo v. Bell* 1977; *Quilloin v. Walcott* 1978; *Parham v. Hughes* 1979; *Lehr v. Robertson* 1983).

These decisions demonstrate the Court's reluctance to interfere with a governmental decision to treat men and women differently. They represent "hard cases" because they exemplify the "cultural limits of the equality principle" (Williams 1982, 180), and critics have charged that the Court does not meet the challenge of the

Table 1

Male-Female Equal Protection Cases Since 1971

CASE	DATE	ISSUE	VOTE	+/-**
<u>Reed</u>	1971	Preference for males as estate administrators	9-0	+
<u>Stanley</u>*	1972	Unwed father automatically denied child custody	5-2	+
<u>Frontiero</u>	1973	Right of servicewoman to receive dependent's benefits restricted	8-1	+
<u>Kahn</u>*	1974	Automatic tax exemption for widows	6-3	-
<u>Geduldig</u>	1974	Exclusion of disability payments for normal pregnancy and childbirth	6-3	-
<u>Ballard</u>*	1975	Navy's promotion policy allows longer time in rank for female officers	5-4	-
<u>Wiesenfeld</u>*	1975	Childcare benefits exclusively for widowed mothers	8-0	+
<u>Stanton</u>	1975	Females denied parental support because reach majority earlier	8-1	+
<u>Craig</u>*	1976	Male age of beer purchase higher	7-2	+
<u>Goldfarb</u>*	1977	OASDI benefits restricted to widowers	5-4	+
<u>Webster</u>*	1977	Female preference in elapsed years calculation for OASDI	9-0	-
<u>Vorchheimer</u>	1977	Public high school restricted to males	4-4	-
<u>Fiallo</u>*	1977	Immigration preference restricted to mothers of illegitimate children	6-3	-

Quilloin*	1978	Unmarried father unable to veto adoption of illegitimate child	9-0	-
Orr*	1979	Alimony restricted to husbands	6-3	+
Parham*	1979	Only mother can sue for wrongful death of illegitimate child	5-4	-
Caban*	1979	Unmarried father unable to veto adoption of illegitimate child	5-4	+
Westcott***	1979	AFDC benefits only to families of unemployed fathers	9-0	+
Wengler*	1980	Worker compensation benefits to widowers restricted	8-1	+
Kirchberg	1981	Husband's right to unilaterally dispose of community property	9-0	+
Michael M.*	1981	Criminal liability for statutory rape restricted to males	5-4	-
Rostker*	1981	Only males subject to draft registration	6-3	-
Hogan*	1982	State University nursing school restricted to females only	5-4	+
Lehr*	1983	Notice to unmarried father in adoption proceedings of illegitimate child restricted	6-3	-
Mathews*	1984	Pension offset imposed upon nondependent males	9-0	-

* cases brought by males

** + = gender classification struck
- = gender classification upheld

*** case brought jointly by husband and wife

"hard" cases because it fails to disentangle physiological sex differences from societal gender norms and because it readily accepts superficial justifications for laws implicating biological sex differences (see Law 1984; MacKinnon 1979; and Williams 1982).

A NEW DIRECTION FOR REVIEW OF LEGISLATIVE CLASSIFICATIONS

These cases highlight two flaws in the Court's approach to equal protection: First, the Court sanctions questionable compensatory legislation that perpetuates gender stereotypes, and, second and more importantly, it approves of laws based upon physical differences that validate and reinforce cultural biases and role prescriptions. Eliminating these errors requires a stricter review of legislative classifications. Under strict scrutiny, virtually all legislative gender distinctions would be eliminated and, where laws are validly based on physical differences, there would be a judgment made about whether the law is the least restrictive alternative to achieving the desired end, a common inquiry under strict scrutiny review.[7]

A fundamental tenet of equal protection doctrine is that the level of scrutiny is virtually outcome-determinative. Over the years, strict scrutiny has meant that in the typical racial classification (without a benign or compensatory purpose) no law is acceptable. This stems from the language and mind-set accompanying strict scrutiny review, which derives from the presumption of unconstitutionality attached to the legislation.

Strict scrutiny aims at preventing overinclusive or underinclusive legislative classifications.[8] It requires a virtually airtight fit between the classification and the legislative purpose so that "any degree of avoidable overinclusiveness or underinclusiveness would be deemed 'too much'" (Fiss 1976, 113-114). The tightness of the fit can be ascertained by asking whether the statute as written (not the state's *post hoc* justification) can be logically applied to both sexes—that is, whether one can substitute "male" for "female" (and vice versa) in the wording of the statute without reducing it to a physical impossibility. If the substitution can be made, the classification is overinclusive or underinclusive and is therefore unacceptable.

It is especially important to subject to this test laws that purportedly are based upon physical differences. Insisting upon a tight fit between the legislative goal and the classification ensures that the law is based upon actual physical differences and does not merely reinforce cultural stereotypes. Aside from *Geduldig*, the classifications thus far upheld by the Court would have been struck down under this standard.

For policy-making purposes, the fit would only be perfect for childbearing differences between the sexes. Policies such as childcare leave for women only, premised upon stereotypical or culturally derived notions of male and female behavior, should be eliminated at this stage of the review. The major unanswered question concerns the legitimacy of a law offering a pregnancy leave policy that obviously benefits women only.

THE DEBATE OVER PREFERENTIAL TREATMENT OF PREGNANCY

In the past, the Court allowed states to enact pregnancy legislation that was, for the most part, "synonymous with unfavorable treatment" (Williams 1982, 193). The Court often failed to perceive "that some of the legal rules restricting the activities of pregnant women were not required by physiology, but resulted from a social order built on patriarchal principles, designed to protect the family as a reproductive institution" (Rubin 1986, 77-78). The challenge in pregnancy legislation is to differentiate between laws that restrict options for women and laws that expand them.

Not sanguine about the ability to meet this challenge, Williams argues against all laws relating to pregnancy, because, she maintains, one cannot make principled distinctions between special treatment in favor of pregnant women and special treatment against them. The safest way, she thinks, is to refrain from legislating in the area at all, and she urges that pregnancy be equated to "other physical conditions that may affect workers" (1982, 193).

Similarly, Kirp, Yudof, and Franks (1986, 109) see maternity benefits in the 1980s as a modern version of the protective legislation of the early 1900s. They would remove all laws interfering with a free market approach to pregnancy. They argue that, "unlike other disabilities covered by employee health plans, pregnancy is usually voluntary and welcome [and] because the medical costs associated with normal pregnancy are relatively low, the ordinary family can usually plan for them."

This "equality" or hands-off approach fails to acknowledge that pregnancy imposes special obstacles on women in the work force. Treating men and women equally with respect to pregnancy minimizes the burdens that child bearing imposes upon working women. "Leave policies that define normal conditions of employment in terms inadequate to accommodate pregnancy define pregnancy as incompatible with employment. Such policies do not merely embody normative assumptions about the sexes; they perpetuate them" (Employment Equality Under the Pregnancy Discrimination Act of 1978, 1985, 942). The equality approach that allows pregnancy benefits to be equated with disability benefits sends the wrong message; it portrays pregnancy as a workplace oddity rather than a brief interlude in a woman's employment history.[9]

Legislation embodying a preferential treatment approach for pregnancy, already enacted in varying form in states such as Connecticut, Hawaii, Kansas, and Washington, should encompass at least such measures as a minimum pregnancy leave with pay, guarantees of job retention with accumulated seniority upon return, and health insurance coverage during the leave.[10]

Provisions such as these acknowledge the reality of the financial and physical burdens of pregnancy on working women without penalizing them for it. Policies providing nutritional programs for pregnant women, as well as a more expanded version of government-provided health care for women not currently working, should also receive constitutional approval.

Preferential pregnancy measures are hardly novel as social welfare policy; they are widespread throughout the world. Every industrialized country in the world, except the United States, as well as a number of developing nations—75 nations in all—provide some sort of maternity or parental benefits that cover all or part of a worker's salary and health costs related to pregnancy (Employment Equality Under the Pregnancy Discrimination Act of 1978, 1985, 942, n. 64).

PREGNANCY LEGISLATION AND THE COURT

The Court's present view of pregnancy-related legislation, reflected in its interpretation of the Pregnancy Discrimination Act (PDA) of 1978, demonstrates some of the problems associated with an equality approach. The Act, an amendment to Title VII of the 1964 Civil Rights Act stating that "women affected by pregnancy . . . shall be treated the same for all employment-related purposes," has become the primary yardstick for measuring the legality of pregnancy legislation.

The PDA was enacted to overrule the Supreme Court's decision in *General Electric v. Gilbert* (1976), which held that Title VII allowed pregnancy disability benefits to be excluded from a female worker's package of benefits. While the Act equated pregnancy discrimination with sex discrimination, it did not specify the permissible bounds of a pregnancy policy—that is, whether it should serve as a "floor" or a "ceiling" for pregnancy benefits.

The first case decided under the PDA, *Newport News v. EEOC* (1983), maintained the evenhanded approach by merely requiring the extension of existing maternity benefits to the wives of *male* employees.

In *California Savings and Loan v. Guerra* (1987) the Court narrowly ruled that the California law requiring employers to provide unpaid leave and reinstatement to pregnant employees was not preempted by the PDA. The Court held that employers could adhere to both the California law and Title VII by providing similar benefits to all employees.

Even though *Guerra* upheld the law, it is unlikely that it disposed of the issue. It was decided by a 6-3 vote over the dissent of Justices White and Powell and of Chief Justice Rehnquist, who wrote that the language of the PDA "leaves no room for preferential treatment of pregnant workers." Moreover, Justice Stevens' concurring opinion left open the question of whether other forms of preference for pregnancy might be inconsistent with the goals of Title VII, and Justice Scalia concurred on the narrow ground that *this particular* state law did not directly conflict with Title VII.

A week after *Guerra* was decided, the Supreme Court refused to affirm or to strike down a Montana statute that required reasonable maternity leave and job reinstatement. Instead, in *Miller-Wohl v. Montana Commissioner of Labor and Industry* (1987), the Court remanded the case to the Montana court for review in light of *Guerra*.

Finally, although not a PDA case, *Wimberly v. Missouri Labor and Industrial Relations Commission* (1987) is another example of a nondiscriminatory—evenhanded—approach to pregnancy. Here, a woman was not rehired after taking pregnancy leave. Her unemployment claim was denied on the grounds that she had left work voluntarily and without good cause. Ruling that the State did not violate the 1976 Federal Unemployment Tax Act that prohibits the denial of unemployment compensation "solely on the basis of pregnancy," the Court declared that the Federal Tax Act only intended to prohibit states from singling out pregnancy for unfavorable treatment. Missouri's denial of her unemployment compensation was not based upon her pregnancy and therefore was not illegal under the statute.

PREGNANCY BENEFITS AS AFFIRMATIVE ACTION

This analysis would be incomplete without at least a brief consideration of the constitutional arguments that may be offered in support of preferential pregnancy legislation within the paradigm of strict scrutiny review. Constitutional review of preferential pregnancy legislation can be analogized to review of compensatory racial classifications. Although the Supreme Court applies strict scrutiny to *all* racial laws, it has nevertheless adopted an approach to affirmative action that allows race to be taken into account as a compensatory measure under narrowly defined circumstances.

Rejecting the argument that benign racial classifications should be reviewed more leniently, in *University of California v. Bakke* (1978), a plurality opinion by Justice Powell extended strict scrutiny to benign racial classifications as well.[11] Yet, even using strict scrutiny, the Court has approved racial classifications to eradicate the effects of racial discrimination in education (*Swann v. Charlotte-Mecklenburg* 1971) and in voting (*UJO v. Carey* 1977) and has allowed race to be a factor in admissions to state universities (*Bakke*).[12] More recently, in *U.S. v. Paradise* (1987) the Court held that a 50% promotion plan for black state troopers in Alabama was constitutionally valid because it was justified by a compelling state interest and was narrowly tailored to serve its purpose. *Paradise* shows that even when the Court uses the language of strict scrutiny, in benign classifications, the review is not always "fatal in fact."

As the Court explained in *Wygant v. Jackson* (1986), an important factor in assessing the constitutionality of benign classifications is the potential harm done to innocent parties, that is, those not guilty of discrimination. Because both sexes contribute to the condition at hand, there are no "innocent" parties to be harmed in pregnancy benefits legislation (Kirp and Robyn 1979, 955).

Additionally, said the Court, the means chosen by the state—that is, the classification—must be narrowly tailored to achieve the objective sought. This step in the strict scrutiny analysis is also relevant to an assessment of whether the legislation impacts adversely upon women by "protecting" them out of jobs or promotions. While it is not always possible to predict the impact of legislation, a limited remedy based upon the sex-based characteristic of pregnancy should survive judicial scrutiny. Pregnancy benefits restricted to child bearing and not extending to child rearing are sufficiently tailored and can be justified by the state's compelling interest in alleviating the disadvantages imposed upon women in the work force by pregnancy as well as its interest in maternal health.

CLOSING ARGUMENT

An equality or parity approach places the burdens of pregnancy solely on women and does not acknowledge that most workers, especially women workers, have limited bargaining power over employee benefits. One has only to think of prototypical female workers—a nonunion blue-collar worker in a North Carolina textile mill, a nurse's aide in a small-town hospital, or a pink-collar employee in a small office or restaurant—to realize the shortsightedness of a parity approach. Insisting upon parity between men and women ignores the legitimate needs of pregnant women workers.

The workplace is currently adapted to the male experience of reproduction and family life; merely treating pregnant women like disabled men is not an adequate solution to changing this focus.

Insisting upon equality or parity of treatment between men and women transmits a message to women that they are less essential to the workplace than men. While some argue that it is preferable to have *no* pregnancy legislation at all, the Court should accept remedial measures under strictly controlled conditions. The marginality of women workers is exacerbated by the refusal to accommodate the needs of pregnant women, and failure to enact beneficial legislation perpetuates the inequality of the work force.

Policies recognizing the special status of pregnancy are necessary to achieve equality in society, because they play a critical role in allowing women to become fully integrated members of the work force. However, pregnancy benefits are not for women alone; they advantage society in a number of ways. Giving women preferential treatment during pregnancy, which enables them to combine parenthood and employment, increases their attachment to the work force. Moreover, preferential pregnancy legislation apportions the cost of children more equally within society. Just as the political system has recognized the need for a shared responsibility for the elderly through retirement benefits and medical care, it must also recognize the need for shared responsibility in the welfare of the woman worker. Accommodating the special needs of working women through medical care provisions and alleviating work responsibilities for the limited period of time affected by the pregnancy are important steps toward realizing this goal.

Pregnancy benefits should not be foresworn for the sake of an equality theory that ignores the legitimate needs of pregnant women; legislative initiatives to benefit pregnant women can receive the Court's blessing under strict scrutiny analysis as well as under the antidiscrimination provisions of Title VII.

NOTES

1. I am grateful to an anonymous reviewer who stressed the importance of making this distinction clear.

2. A caveat must be added: The arguments offered here are not predicated upon the likelihood of such legislation; rather they are designed to provide a theoretical framework for the Court to approve such legislation should it be enacted.

3. These cases were identified by reviewing all Supreme Court sex- and gender-based cases since 1971. Of the 25 cases complaining of equal protection viola-

tions, some were decided by the Court on due process grounds and some on both equal protection and due process grounds.

4. These two categories include 11 of the 12 cases in which the Court upheld the gender distinction; the twelfth case is *Vorchheimer v. School District of Philadelphia* (1977), in which the Court affirmed, by an equally divided Court, the lower court decision that attendance at a public high school may be restricted to males only. Only two of the 12 cases (*Vorchheimer* and *Geduldig v. Aiello* [1974]) were brought by women.

5. *Ballard* arguably does not belong in this category, but, like the other compensation cases, the gender classification in *Ballard* was based upon the need to compensate women for "discrimination" against them.

6. In these cases the Supreme Court accepted laws of dubious worth in compensating women for past discrimination—especially when weighed against the burden of enshrining gender distinctions in the law. The law in *Webster* had already expired, the benefits in *Mathews* were statutorily limited to five years, and the property tax exemption in *Kahn* amounted to 15 dollars a year. Moreover, these decisions reflected an acceptance of the underlying discrimination against women (see Gertner 1979).

7. In *Frontiero v. Richardson* (1973) there were four votes to impose strict scrutiny on gender classifications. Justice Powell, joined by Justice Blackman and Chief Justice Burger, concurred in the judgment only because of a reluctance to adopt such a wide-sweeping rule in gender classifications. They felt that the Court should not preempt the political process that was then debating the ratification of the Equal Rights Amendment. Ratification of the ERA would have had the same effect as imposing strict scrutiny. Obviously, the ERA was not ratified and is not likely to be in the near future. Thus my argument here is that, of the two methods of imposing searching review of laws pertaining to male-female differences, the more likely solution lies in the Court's adoption of strict scrutiny. That the Court seems to have moved closer to this position can be seen in the language of the 1982 case, *Mississippi University v. Hogan*, in which Justice O'Connor stated that gender classifications now required "exceedingly important justifications."

8. "Underinclusiveness" refers to legislation that excludes a class of persons that should be included within the benefits or burdens of the statute. "Overinclusiveness" refers to legislation that includes a class of persons that should not be included within the reach of the legislation. The statute in *Kahn v. Shevin* (1974) illustrates both underinclusiveness and overinclusiveness. It was overinclusive because it provided tax relief for wealthy widows and underinclusive because it failed to provide benefits for needy widowers.

9. Government figures show that in 1985 there were 51,050,000 women in the civilian labor force out of a total civilian labor force of 115,461,000 (*Employment and Earnings* July 1985); 54.5% of all women were in the workforce in 1985, and about 70% of women aged 20 to 44 were in the labor force (*Monthly Labor Review* November 1985). The data also show that in 1984, for every 1,000 women between the ages of 16 and 44, there were 65.4 live births (*Vital Statistics of the United States*).

10. The proposed Parental and Disability Leave Act of 1985 would have required employers subject to Title VII to grant covered employees a specified number of weeks of unpaid disability or parental leave. Renamed the Family and Medical Leave Act of 1986, the bill has not been enacted to date. In 1987 a compromise bill emerged in committee that sharply reduced benefits available under the Act; these benefits fall short of the kind of benefits envisioned in this study.

11. The Court recently affirmed this position in *City of Richmond v. Croson* (1989).

12. The Court explained in *Bakke* that the courts were required to make a finding of past racial discrimination under strict scrutiny before fashioning a remedy based upon race.

REFERENCES

Baer, Judith A. 1983. *Equality Under the Constitution*. Ithaca, NY: Cornell University Press.

Caban v. Mohammed. 1979. 441 U.S. 380.

Califano v. Goldfarb. 1977. 430 U.S. 199.

Califano v. Webster. 1977. 430 U.S. 313.

Califano v. Westcott. 1979. 443 U.S. 76.

California Federal Savings and Loan Association v. Guerra. 1987. 106 S.Ct. 783.

City of Richmond v. Croson. 1989. 109 S.Ct. 706.

Craig v. Boren. 1976. 429 U.S. 190.

"Employment Equality Under the Pregnancy Discrimination Act of 1978." 1985. *Yale Law Journal* 94:929-956.

Fiallo v. Bell. 1977. 430 U.S. 787.

Fiss, Owen. 1976. "Groups and the Equal Protection Clause." *Philosophy and Public Affairs* 5:107-177.

Frontiero v. Richardson. 1973. 411 U.S. 677.

Geduldig v. Aiello. 1974. 417 U.S. 484.

General Electric Company v. Gilbert. 1976. 429 U.S. 125.

Gertner, Nancy. 1979. "*Bakke* on Affirmative Action for Women: Pedestal or Cage?" *Harvard Civil Rights-Civil Liberties Law Review* 14:175-214.

Ginsburg, Ruth Bader. 1978. "Some Thoughts on Benign Classification in the Context of Sex." *Connecticut Law Review* 10:813-827.

Gunther, Gerald. 1972. "Foreword: In Search of Evolving Doctrine on a Changing Court: A Model for a Newer Equal Protection." *Harvard Law Review* 86:1-48.

Heckler v. Mathews. 1984. 465 U.S. 728.

Kahn v. Shevin. 1974. 416 U.S. 351.

Kirchberg v. Feenstra. 1981. 450 U.S. 455.

Kirp, David, and Dorothy Robyn. 1979. "Pregnancy, Justice and the Justices." *Texas Law Review* 57:947-964.

Kirp, David, Mark Yudof, and Marlene Strong Franks. 1986. *Gender Justice*. Chicago: University of Chicago Press.

Law, Sylvia. 1984. "Rethinking Sex and the Constitution." *University of Pennsylvania Law Review* 132:955-1040.

Lehr v. Robertson. 1983. 463 U.S. 248.

Lerner, Gerda. 1986. *The Creation of Patriarchy*. Oxford: Oxford University Press.

MacKinnon, Catharine. 1979. *Sexual Harassment of Working Women*. New Haven, CT: Yale University Press.

Michael M. v. Superior Court. 1981. 450 U.S. 464.

Miller-Wohl Company v. Montana Commissioner of Labor and Industry. 1987. 107 S.Ct. 919.

Mississippi University for Women v. Hogan. 1982. 458 U.S. 718.

National Center for Health Statistics. 1985. *Vital Statistics of the United States*. Rockville, MD: U.S. Department of Health, Education, and Welfare.

Newport News Shipbuilding and Dry Dock v. EEOC. 1983. 462 U.S. 669.

Orr v. Orr. 1979. 440 U.S. 268.

Parham v. Hughes. 1979. 441 U.S. 347.

Quilloin v. Walcott. 1978. 434 U.S. 246.

Reed v. Reed. 1971. 404 U.S. 71.

Regents of the University of California v. Bakke. 1978. 438 U.S. 265.

Rostker v. Goldberg. 1981. 453 U.S. 57.

Rubin, Eva. 1986. *The Supreme Court and the American Family*. Westport, CT: Greenwood Press.

Schlesinger v. Ballard. 1975. 419 U.S. 498.

Stanley v. Illinois. 1972. 405 U.S. 645.

Stanton v. Stanton. 1975. 421 U.S. 7.

Swann v. Charlotte-Mecklenburg Board of Education. 1971. 402 U.S. 1.

United Jewish Organizations v. Carey. 1977. 430 U.S. 144.

United States v. Paradise. 1987. 107 S.Ct. 1053.

U.S. Bureau of Labor Statistics. July 1985. *Employment and Earnings*. Washington, D.C.: U.S. Department of Labor.

U.S. Bureau of Labor Statistics. November 1985. *Monthly Labor Review*. Washington, D.C.: U.S. Department of Labor.

Vorchheimer v. School District of Philadelphia. 1977. 532 F.2d 880 (3d Cir. 1976), aff'd by an equally divided Court, 430 U.S. 703.

Weinberger v. Wiesenfeld. 1975. 420 U.S. 636.

Wengler v. Druggists Mutual Insurance Co. 1980. 446 U.S. 142.

Williams, Wendy. Spring 1982. "The Equality Crisis: Some Reflections on Culture, Courts and Feminism." *Women's Rights Law Reporter* 7:175-200.

Wimberly v. Labor and Industrial Relations Commission of Missouri. 1987. 107 S.Ct. 821.

Wygant v. Jackson Board of Education. 1986. 106 S.Ct. 1842.

Gender Difference and Gender Disadvantage

Deborah L. Rhode

SUMMARY. This paper explores the theoretical foundations of American sex discrimination law. Traditional legal frameworks have analyzed gender issues in terms of gender difference. Yet, under this approach, sex-based differences have been both overlooked and overvalued. In some instances, such as occupational restrictions and military service, courts have transformed biological distinctions into cultural imperatives. In other cases, such as those involving pregnancy, sex-based differences have remained unacknowledged and unaddressed. The alternative framework proposed here focuses less on gender difference than on gender disadvantage—on inequalities in the sexes' social status, political power, and economic security. Taking issues surrounding occupational restrictions, protective labor, and maternity policies as representative examples, the paper suggests how a contextual inquiry can usefully shift gender discrimination law from its focus on difference to the consequences that follow from it.

For most of this nation's history, the law's approach to gender difference has alternated between exaggeration and neglect. Neglect has been the preferred strategy; the recent cluster of Bicentennial conferences on women and the Constitution is an ironic reminder of that fact.[1] When the nation's founding fathers spoke of "We the People" they were not using the term generically. Although subject to the Constitution's mandates, women were unacknowledged in its text, uninvited in its formulation, unsolicited in its ratification, and, before the last quarter-century, largely uninvolved in its interpretation. Yet, as these recent conferences also testify, such patterns of silence have been broken. Women have found a voice. How we should use it is a question worthy of greater exploration.

The following analysis considers a specific set of questions about voice. How we describe the relation between the sexes involves a

Deborah L. Rhode is affiliated with Stanford University.

politics of paradigms that legal decision makers rarely acknowledge or address. For the most part, traditional legal frameworks have analyzed gender issues in terms of gender difference. Under this approach, sex-based distinctions have been both overvalued and overlooked. In some contexts, such as occupational restrictions, courts have transformed biological differences into cultural imperatives. In other cases, such as those involving pregnancy, those differences have remained unrecognized. Significant progress will require an alternative framework, one focused not on gender difference but on gender disadvantage.

PART ONE

Traditional equal protection doctrine has developed within an Aristotelian tradition that defines equality as similar treatment for those who are similarly situated. Under this approach, discrimination presents no difficulties if the groups concerned are dissimilar in some sense that is related to valid regulatory objectives. This analytic paradigm has proven inadequate in both theory and practice. As a theoretical matter, it tends toward tautology; it permits different treatment for those who are different with respect to legitimate purposes, but it provides no criteria for determining what differences matter and what counts as legitimate. As a practical matter, this approach has generated results that are indeterminate, inconsistent, and often indefensible.

The alternative proposed here would shift emphasis from gender difference to gender disadvantage. This approach builds on the work of other feminist legal scholars including Katherine Bartlett (1987, 1988), Mary Becker (1987), Clare Dalton, Lucina Finley, Ann Freedman (1983), Mary Jo Frug (1979), Kenneth Karst (1984), Herma Hill Kay, Sylvia Law (1984), Christine Littleton (1987), Catharine MacKinnon (1987), Carrie Menkel-Meadow (1985), Martha Minow (1987), Frances Olsen (1983), Ann Scales, Elizabeth Schneider (1986), Nadine Taub, Robin West, and Wendy Williams. By focusing on disadvantage, such an approach responds to the two most prevalent strands of feminist jurisprudence, those that stress women's fundamental equality with men and those that seek accommodation of women's differences.

Under this alternative paradigm, a determination that the sexes are not "similarly situated" only begins the discussion. Analysis would then turn on whether legal recognition of sex-based differences is more likely to reduce or to reinforce sex-based disparities in political power, social status, and economic security. Such an approach would entail a more searching review than has generally been apparent in cases involving gender. Its focus would extend beyond the rationality of means and legitimacy of ends. Rather, this alternative would require that governmental objectives include a substantive commitment to gender equality—to a society in which women as a group are not disadvantaged in controlling their own destiny.

This paradigm presupposes a better understanding of the harms of sex-based classifications, the diversity of women's interests, and the complexities of strategies designed to address them. Subsequent discussion of issues such as military service exemptions, protective labor legislation, and maternity and parental leaves provides representative illustrations of these complexities. Preferential policies that offer concrete advantages to some women in the short term may carry a less obvious price in the long term. Sex-based classifications often reinforce sex-based stereotypes and thus help to perpetuate sex-based inequalities.

In these cases, any adequate legal analysis will require close attention to context. Shifting focus from gender difference to gender disadvantage will not always supply definitive answers, but it can at least suggest the right questions. Which women benefit, by how much, and at what cost? Reframing the issue in these terms can also point up the limitations of traditional strategies, which too often have promised equality in form but not in fact. If we are to make significant progress, our goal must include not simply access to, but alteration of, existing social institutions (Littleton 1987; Rhode 1986; Taub and Williams 1986).

PART TWO

Until the last two decades, American lawmakers have generally leapt from the fact of sex-based differences to the appropriateness of differential treatment, often without the benefit of any intermediate premises. In contexts ranging from tax exemptions to criminal penalties, judges have found it "too plain for discussion" that "real differences" between men and women justified their different legal status (*Platt v. Commonwealth* 1926, 914, 915; *Quong Wing v. Kirkendall* 1912, 59, 63). It has been less plain, however, which way those differences cut. So, for example, women's "special" attributes have pointed to different results on identical issues—to both longer and shorter prison terms, and to both favored and disfavored treatment in child custody determinations (compare *Commonwealth v. Daniels* 1967; *Ex Parte Gosselin* 1945; Olsen 1984; *Territory v. Armstrong* 1924; and *Wark v. State* 1970).

In some contexts, decision makers have attributed such sex-based differences to nature, and in other contexts to nurture, but most often they have confused the two. The most celebrated examples have involved occupational contexts in which exclusively male decision makers have contemplated the boundaries of their own exclusivity. Throughout the late nineteenth and early twentieth centuries, many judges identified a "Law of Nature" or of "the Creator" that decreed domesticity as woman's only destiny (*Bradwell v. State* 1872, 130, 137 [Bradley, concurring]). Women's "proper delicacy," "tender sensibilities," and maternal responsibilities served as disqualifications for a diverse range of occupations ranging from practicing law to shining shoes (Baer 1978; Baker 1976; *Bradwell v. State* 1872; *In the Matter of Goodell* 1878). Although the Lord's will ultimately was reversed in most of these contexts, the legacy of the difference framework lingers on. The most recent illustrations have involved women's exclusion from occupational settings thought to present special demands or risks, such as military combat, maximum security prisons, or toxic work sites.

A difference-oriented framework copes poorly with circumstances in which the sexes are not similarly situated. The Court's 1981 decision upholding a male-only draft registration system is a case in point: In this case a majority of Justices reverted to the time-honored technique of avoiding difficulties by avoiding the issue. The Court simply assumed that differences between the sexes justified differences in combat eligibility and that these differences further justified exemptions from registration requirements (*Rostker v. Goldberg* 1981). Evidence concerning women's effective performance in a wide range of noncombat and combat-related contexts here and abroad was diplomatically ignored. Nor did the Court consider the availability of gender-neutral standards to screen for positions requiring special physical strength (Kornblum 1984; *Rostker v. Goldberg* 1981). What was perhaps most telling was the absence of any concern about the stereotypes underpinning combat exemptions: for example, legislators' assumptions that women could not and men would not fight well in mixed units, that sexual proximity would breed sexual promiscuity, that the nation would be reluctant to mobilize if its daughters were at risk, and that the trauma of gender-integrated field latrines would hamstring the infantry (Estrich and Kerr 1984; Rhode 1983; Ruddick 1984).

How actively to demand the benefits and burdens of military service has been a matter of considerable controversy within the women's movement. Among some constituencies the goal is to end conscription for both sexes, not to allocate its burdens equally. For these feminists, women's traditional ethics of nurturance are fundamentally at odds with the ethics of aggression that have traditionally shaped American defense policy. Yet other feminists, while agreeing with the need for changes in military structures and service requirements, view women's equal participation as a means to that end. As they note, restrictions of women in combat have long served to limit women's access to desirable jobs, training, and benefits and to reinforce traditional notions of masculine aggression and female passivity (Kornblum 1984; Williams 1982). However one assesses the practical effects of full female participation in the military, there remain profound symbolic reasons to seek that objective. It is difficult for women to attain equal treatment and equal respect as citizens while remaining exempt from one of citizenship's central responsibilities.

Similar points are applicable in other occupational contexts. A recurring issue has involved interpretations of Title VII of the Civil Rights Act, which prohibits discrimination on the basis of sex except where it is a "bona fide occupational qualification" (BFOQ). On the whole, courts have interpreted this exception narrowly, but the circumstances where it has survived point up limitations in difference-oriented paradigms.

The first BFOQ case to reach the Supreme Court involved an employment policy that barred job applications from women, but not men, with preschool children. In a brief opinion written in 1970, the Supreme Court effectively avoided decision by remanding the case to lower courts for two determinations—whether conflicting family obligations were demonstrably more relevant to job performance for a woman than for a man, and, if so, whether that would constitute a BFOQ defense to the employer's policy (*Phillips v. Martin Marietta* 1970). Yet, by asking only whether the sexes were different in a sense that is relevant to this differential treatment, the Court ignored more fundamental issues about the legitimacy of that treatment and of the gender stereotypes underlying it. In effect, the Court ignored the social costs of penalizing individuals for their parental status and of visiting those penalties disproportionately on mothers.

Nor was the Supreme Court's next pronouncement on BFOQs a substantial improvement. At issue were Alabama prison regulations preventing women from serving as guards in positions requiring close physical contact with inmates. In upholding such restrictions, the majority relied on "substantial" trial testimony indicating that women would pose a "substantial" security problem because of their special vulnerability to sexual assault (*Dothard v. Rawlinson* 1977). The factual basis for that testimony was somewhat less substantial. Never did the state explain why *sexual* assaults, as opposed to assaults in general, posed a particular threat to prison safety. Nor did the Court explain its refusal to credit equally substantial evidence indicating that properly trained female guards had not presented risks in other state maximum security prisons. By adopting what Catharine MacKinnon has characterized as the "reasonable rapist" perspective on employment opportunities, the majority decision perpetuated stereotypes of women's inability to protect themselves (MacKinnon 1987; Williams 1982). The Court's reasoning also penalized female job applicants for the "barbaric" prison conditions that allegedly placed them at risk.

If this difference-oriented approach to occupational qualifications remains unchallenged, it could have serious consequences for both men and women in potentially toxic workplaces. In the interests of maternal and fetal health, courts have sanctioned layoffs of pregnant employees or bans on employing fertile women. Since an estimated 20 million jobs may pose some reproductive risks, many of which affect men as well as women, it is crucial for decision makers to focus less on gender differences and more on gender disadvantages (Becker 1986; EEOC 1980; Williams 1981). The strategy must be to reduce employment hazards, not to restrict female employment opportunities.

PART THREE

One final context in which the advantages of shifting paradigms is most apparent involves special treatment in protective labor and maternity policies. The issue arose around the turn of this century as increasing numbers of state legislatures began passing regulations governing maximum hours, minimum wages, and working conditions. Controversies increased after a pair of Supreme Court decisions struck down such regulations for male workers as a violation of their freedom to contract but upheld restrictions for female employees in light of their special vulnerabilities and reproductive responsibilities (*Lochner v. New York* 1905; *Muller v. Oregon* 1908). Even after the Supreme Court reversed its holding as to male workers, the disputes over gender-specific protections persisted. In part, the debate centered on concerns about the fate of such protections under a proposed constitutional Equal Rights Amendment. Underlying that issue were deeper questions about mandates guaranteeing formal equality in circumstances of social inequality.

Those same questions have resurfaced in the last decade as the women's movement has divided over the merits of special protection for maternity leave. Then, as now, feminists who supported gender-specific policies began from the premise that women have special needs that justify special regulatory intervention. Earlier in the century the focus was on female employees' unequal labor force status and unequal domestic burdens. Most women workers were crowded into low-paying jobs with few advancement opportunities and little likelihood of improving their situation through unionization. Female employees were also far more likely than their male counterparts to assume major family responsibilities, and the combination of those duties with prevailing 12- to 14-hour work shifts imposed enormous hardships. For most of these women, statutory regulation of hours and wages meant a substantial improvement in their quality of life (Baer 1978; Baker 1976; Cott 1987; Women's Bureau 1928). Yet, as feminists who opposed gender-specific statutes also noted, such protections, by making women more expensive, often protected them out of any jobs desirable to male competitors. In some contexts, regulation also increased female unemployment and reinforced stereotypes about men's breadwinning and women's nurturing roles (Baer 1978; Kessler-Harris 1980; Landes 1980).

Although those on both sides of the protective labor debate claimed to speak for women, women's interests were more divided than partisans acknowledged. For the majority of workers, clustered in female-dominated jobs, gender-specific regulation resulted in significant improvements. Yet the price was to limit other employment opportunities and thus to reinforce the social inequalities that protective statutes could not adequately address. Moreover, the ideology of protectionism and of women's maternal mission spilled over to other contexts in which protection was less advantageous (Johnston and Knapp 1971; Olsen 1986; Williams 1985).

The contemporary debate about maternity policies involves similar claims and presents similar complexities. The issue has its origins in the Supreme Court's initial confusion over how to treat pregnancy. What makes the pregnancy cases particularly instructive as sex discrimination opinions was the Supreme Court's unwillingness to treat them as such. During the mid-1970s, a majority of Justices upheld policies providing employee benefits for virtually all medical treatment except that related to childbirth. Yet, in the first of these cases, the Court relegated the entire discussion of discrimination to a footnote in which the majority announced its somewhat novel conclusion that pregnancy policies did not even involve "gender as such" (*Geduldig v. Aiello* 1974, n. 21); rather, employers were simply drawing a distinction between—in the Court's memorable terminology—"pregnant women" and "non-pregnant persons."

Preoccupied with issues of difference rather than disadvantage, the majority perceived no issue of discrimination. Since pregnancy was a "unique" and "additional" disability for women, employers were entitled to exclude it from insurance coverage (Bartlett 1974; *Geduldig v. Aiello* 1974; *General Electric Co. v. Gilbert* 1976).

Never did the Court explain why only pregnancy was "unique" while men's disabilities, such as prostatectomies, were fully covered. Rather, the Court's characterization assumed what should have been at issue and made the assumption from a male reference point. Men's physiology set the standard, against which women's claims appeared only "additional."

In the aftermath of these cases, concerted lobbying efforts prompted passage of the federal Pregnancy Discrimination Act, which provided that pregnancy should be treated "the same as" other medical risks for employment-related purposes (92 Stat. 2076). This remains, however, one of the many contexts in which equality in form has not resulted in equality in fact. The Act requires only that employers treat pregnancy like other disabilities. It does not affirmatively require adequate disability policies. In the absence of statutory mandates, such policies have been slow to develop. Data from the late 1980s indicate that about three-fifths of female workers were not entitled to wage replacement and a third could not count on returning to the same job after a normal period of leave. The United States has remained alone among major industrialized nations in failing to provide such benefits (Congressional Caucus for Women's Issues 1986; Kamerman and Kahn 1987). A difference-oriented approach that is focused on formal, not substantive, equality does nothing to challenge or change the situation.

These inadequacies in national policy have prompted some state initiatives, including legislation that requires employers to provide job-protected leaves for pregnancy but not for other disabilities or for parental and caretaking responsibilities. During the early 1980s, litigation challenging such preferential policies once again found feminists on both sides of the issues. In *California Federal Savings and Loan v. Guerra* (1987) the Supreme Court held that the Pregnancy Discrimination Act's requirement that pregnancy be treated "the same" as other medical disabilities did not bar states from mandating special maternity leaves. Any alternative decision would, in the majority's view, violate the Act's central purpose: to secure workplace equality for women.

Feminists who have argued in favor of such a holding generally begin from the premise that women are unequally situated with respect to reproduction. While no-leave policies pose hardships for both sexes concerning the disabilities they share, those policies present an additional burden for women. As a matter of principle, pregnancy should not have to seem just like other disabilities to obtain protection. As a practical matter, until legislatures are prepared to mandate adequate benefits for all workers, partial coverage seems like an appropriate goal (Finley 1986; Kay 1985; Littleton 1987).

The danger, however, as other feminists have noted, is that settling for the proverbial half a loaf could erode efforts for more comprehensive approaches. To require maternity leaves but not paternity or parental leaves is to reinforce a division of child-rearing responsibilities that has been more separate than equal. Women's unequal family responsibilities translate into unequal career options and perpetuate the socialization patterns on which such inequalities rest. Legislation that makes women more expensive also creates incentives for covert discrimination. Many feminists are unwilling to see women once again "protected" out of jobs desirable to men (National Organization for Women 1987; Williams 1985).

Similar concerns arise with proposals for special slower career paths for working mothers (Schwartz 1989). "Mommy tracks" can too easily become "mommy traps"; they restrict individual opportunity and reinforce sex-based stereotypes. The implication that infants are mothers' responsibility deters men from seeking and employers from accommodating full parental commitment. Such attitudes limit both male and female experience. They impair fathers' formation of nurturing relationships (Chodorow 1978) and force mothers to choose between caretaking commitments and occupational advancement (Rhode 1988).

The value of disadvantage as a legal framework is well illustrated by this debate over maternity policies. For these issues, a sameness/difference approach is utterly unilluminating. Women are both the same and different. They are different in their needs at childbirth but the same in their needs for broader medical, child-rearing, and caretaking policies. To know which side of the sameness/difference dichotomy to emphasize in legal contexts requires some further analytic tool.

A disadvantage-oriented approach focuses on an alternative question: In the current context, what strategy is most likely to serve most women's long-term interests? From this perspective, the preferable strategy for resolving issues such as employee leave policy should be to press for the broadest possible coverage for all workers. While the historical, ideological, and economic consequences of pregnancy should not be overlooked, neither should they be overemphasized. More employers provide job-protected childbirth leaves than other forms of assistance that are equally critical to workers and their dependents. Pregnancy-related policies affect most women workers for relatively brief intervals. The absence of broader disability, health, child-rearing, and caretaking policies remains a chronic problem for the vast majority of employees, male and female, throughout their working lives (Taub 1985; Taub and Williams 1986; Williams 1985).

Even if that problem is assessed solely in economic terms, our current approach appears misguided. As recent estimates have suggested, the social costs resulting from the lack of a national disability policy, in terms of lost earnings, additional public assistance, and reduced productivity, substantially exceed the projected cost of requiring short-term leaves (Spalter-Roth 1988). In this context, both men and women stand to gain if we press for more by refusing to settle for less.

PART FOUR

A framework less concerned with sex-based differences than sex-based disadvantages could expand both our legal and political agendas. The most pressing problems now facing women do not generally find them "similarly situated" to men—poverty, sexual violence, reproductive freedom, family responsibilities. Focusing not on difference but on the difference it makes recasts both the problem and the prescription. In employment settings, the issue becomes not whether gender is relevant to the job as currently structured but how the workplace can be restructured to make gender less relevant. For example, what changes in training programs, working conditions, and cultural attitudes would enable women to exercise authority in military or prison settings? What sorts of public- and private-sector initiatives are necessary to avoid penalizing parenthood? What changes in working schedules, hiring and promotion criteria, leave policies, and child care options would enable both men and women to accommodate home and family responsibilities? (See Kamerman and Kahn 1987; Sidel 1986; and Taub 1985.)

The discourse of difference will sometimes have a place, but it should begin, not end, analysis. As deconstructionists remind us, women are already and always the same and different: the same in their humanity, different in their anatomy. Whichever category we privilege in our legal discourse, the other will always be waiting to disrupt it (Derrida 1977; Silverman 1983). By constantly presenting gender issues in difference-oriented frameworks, conventional legal discourse implicitly biases analysis. To pronounce women either the same or different from men allows men to remain the standard (MacKinnon 1987).

Significant progress toward gender equality will require moving beyond the sameness/difference dilemma. We must insist not just on equal treatment but on woman's treatment as an equal. Such a strategy will require substantial changes in our legal paradigms and social priorities. The stakes are not just equality between the sexes but the quality of life for both of them.

NOTE

1. This paper was delivered at a panel on Gender Difference and Gender Disadvantage at one of these conferences, "Women and the Constitution: A Bicentennial Perspective," sponsored by the Carter Center of Emory University, Georgia State University, and the Carter Library, Atlanta, Georgia, on February 11, 1988. The comments of Barbara Babcock, Peter Chadwick, Nannerl Keohane, Regenia Gagnier, Joanne Martin, Dianne Middlebrook, Robert Post, and Nadine Taub are gratefully acknowledged. A more extended analysis of issues addressed in this paper appears in Rhode (1989) and Rhode (forthcoming).

REFERENCES

Baer, Judith A. 1978. *The Chains of Protection*. West Point, CT: Greenwood Press.

Baker, Elizabeth. 1976. *Protective Labor Legislation*. New York: AMS Press. (Original work published in 1925.)

Bartlett, Katherine. 1974. "Pregnancy and the Constitution: The Uniqueness Trap." *California Law Review* 62:1532.

Bartlett, Katherine. 1987. "MacKinnon's Feminism: Power on What Terms." *California Law Review* 75:1559.

Bartlett, Katherine. 1988. "Review of Feminism Unmodified." *Signs*, 13:879.

Becker, Mary. 1986. "From *Muller v. Oregon* to Fetal Vulnerability Policies." *University of Chicago Law Review* 53:1219-1273.

Becker, Mary. 1987. "Prince Charming: Abstract Equality." *Supreme Court Review* 1987:201-247.

Bradwell v. State. 1872. 83 U.S. 130.

California Federal Savings and Loan Association v. Guerra. 1987. 106 S.Ct. 783.

Chodorow, Nancy. 1978. *The Reproduction of Mothering: Psychoanalysis and the Sociology of Gender*. Berkeley: University of California Press.

Commonwealth v. Daniels. 1967. 210 Pa. Super. 156, 232 A.2d 247, rev'd, 430 Pa. 642, A.2d 400 (1968).

Congressional Caucus for Women's Issues. 1986. Fact Sheet on Parental Leave Legislation. Washington, D.C.: Author.

Cott, Nancy F. 1987. *The Grounding of Modern Feminism*. New Haven, CT: Yale University Press.

Derrida, Jacques. 1977. *Of Grammatology*. Trans. Gayatri Chakravorty Spivak. Baltimore: Johns Hopkins University Press.

Dothard v. Rawlinson. 1977. 433 U.S. 321.

EEOC. February 1, 1980. "Interpretative Guidelines on Employment Discrimination and Reproductive Hazards." 45 *Federal Register* 7514.

Estrich, Susan, and V. Kerr. 1984. "Sexual Justice." In *The Rights of Groups*, ed. Norman Dorsen. New York: ACLU.

Ex Parte Gosselin. 1945. 141 Me. 412, 444 A.2d 882.

Finley, Lucina. 1986. "Transcending Equality Theory: A Way Out of the Maternity and Workplace Debate." *Columbia University Law Review* 86:1118.

Freedman, Ann. 1983. "Sex Equality, Sex Differences and the Supreme Court." *Yale Law Journal* 92:913.

Frug, Mary Jo. 1979. "Securing Job Equality for Women's Labor Market: Hostility to Working Mothers." *Boston University Law Review* 59:55.

Geduldig v. Aiello. 1974. 417 U.S. 484.

General Electric Company v. Gilbert. 1976. 429 U.S. 125.

In the Matter of Goodell. 1878. 39 Wis. 232.

Johnston, John D. Jr., and Charles L. Knapp. 1971. "Sex Discrimination by Law: A Study in Judicial Perspective." *New York University Law Review* 46:675.

Kamerman, Sheila B., and Alfred J. Kahn. 1987. *The Responsive Workplace*. New York: Columbia University Press.

Karst, Kenneth. June 1984. "The Women's Constitution." *Duke Law Journal* 1984:447.

Kay, Herma Hill. 1985. "Equality and Difference: The Case of Pregnancy." *Berkeley Women's Law Journal* 1:1.

Kessler-Harris, Alice. 1980. *Out to Work*. New York: Oxford University Press.

Kornblum, L. 1984. "Women Warriors in a Man's World: The Combat Exclusion." *Law and Inequality: A Journal of Theory and Practice* 2:351.

Landes, E. 1980. "The Effect of State Maximum Hours Laws on the Employment of Women." *Journal of Political Economy* 88:476.

Law, Sylvia. 1984. "Rethinking Sex and the Constitution." *University of Pennsylvania Law Review* 132:955.

Littleton, Christine. 1987. "Reconstructing Sexual Equality." *University of California Law Review* 75:1279.

Lochner v. New York. 1905. 198 U.S. 45.

MacKinnon, Catharine. 1987. *Feminism Unmodified*. Cambridge, MA: Harvard University Press.

Menkel-Meadow, Carrie. 1985. "Portia in a Different Voice." *Berkeley Women's Law Journal* 1:35.

Minow, Martha. 1987. "The Supreme Court 1986 Term: Justice Engendered." *Harvard Law Review* 101:10.

Muller v. Oregon. 1908. 208 U.S. 412.

National Organization for Women. 1987. Brief submitted for *California Federal Savings and Loan Association v. Guerra*. 1987. 106 S.Ct. 783.

Olsen, Frances. 1983. "The Family and the Market: A Study of Ideology and Legal Reform." *Harvard Law Review* 96:1497.

Olsen, Frances. 1984. "The Politics of Family Law." *Law & Inequality* 2:1.

Olsen, Frances. 1986. "From False Paternalism to False Equality: Assaults on Feminist Community: Illinois." *Michigan University Law Journal* 58:869-895.

Phillips v. Martin Marietta Corporation. 1970. 400 U.S. 542.

Platt v. Commonwealth. 1926. 256 Mass. 539, 52 NE 914.

Pregnancy Discrimination Act. October 31, 1978. 92 Stat. 2076, amending 42 U.S.C.A. Section 2000e.

Quong Wing v. Kirkendall, Treasurer of Lewis and Clark County, Montana. 1912. 223 U.S. 59.

Rhode, Deborah L. 1983. "Equal Rights in Retrospect." *Law and Inequality: A Journal of Theory and Practice* 1:1.

Rhode, Deborah L. 1986. "Feminist Perspectives on Legal Ideology." In *What is Feminism*, eds. Juliet Mitchell and Ann Oakley. London: Basil Blackwell.

Rhode, Deborah L. 1988. "Perspectives on Professional Women." *Stanford Law Review* 40:1163.

Rhode, Deborah L. 1989. *Justice and Gender*. Cambridge, MA: Harvard University Press.

Rhode, Deborah L. Forthcoming. *Theoretical Perspectives on Sexual Difference*. New Haven, CT: Yale University Press.

Rostker v. Goldberg. 1981. 353 U.S. 57.

Ruddick, Sarah. 1984. "Women and the Military." *Report From the Center for Philosophy and Public Affairs* 4:3.

Schneider, Elizabeth. 1986. "The Dialectic of Rights and Politics: Perspectives From the Women's Movement." *New York University Law Review* 19:589.

Schwartz, F. 1989. "Management Women and the New Facts of Life." *Harvard Business Review* 65.

Sidel, Ruth. 1986. *Women and Children Last*. New York: Viking.

Silverman, Kaja. 1983. *The Subject of Semiotics*. New York: Oxford University Press.

Spalter-Roth, R. March 1988. *Unnecessary Losses: Costs to Americans for the Lack of Family and Medical Leave*. Washington, D.C.: Institute for Women's Policy Research.

Taub, Nadine. 1985. "From Parental Leaves to Nurturing Leaves." *New York University Review of Law and Social Change* 13:381.

Taub, Nadine, and Wendy Williams. 1986. "Will Equality Require More Than Assimilation, Accommodation, or Separation From the Existing Social Structure?" *Rutgers Law Review* 37:325.

Territory v. Armstrong. 1924. 28 Hawaii 88.

Wark v. State. 1970. 226 A.2d 62 (Maine Sup Ct), cert den. 400 U.S. 952.

Williams, Wendy. 1981. "Firing the Woman to Protect the Fetus: The Reconciliation of Fetal Protection With Employment Opportunity." *Georgetown Law Journal* 69:641.

Williams, Wendy. 1982. "The Equality Crisis: Some Reflections on Culture, Courts, and Feminism." *Women's Rights Law Reporter* 7:1975.

Williams, Wendy. 1985. "Equality's Riddle: Pregnancy and the Equal Treatment-Special Treatment Debate." *New York University Review of Law and Social Change* 13:325.

Women's Bureau. 1928. Bulletin 65, *The Effects of Labor Legislation on the Employment Opportunities of Women*. Washington, D.C.: Government Printing Office.

State Constitutions and Women: Leading or Lagging Agents of Change?

Susan A. MacManus

SUMMARY. This article examines the content and success rate of constitutional changes relating to women's issues that were proposed in the 50 states between 1977 and 1985. Women's issues are defined as those that impact disproportionately on women as a consequence of demographic, socioeconomic, biological, or attitudinal and policy preference patterns. The results show that change proposals benefiting women have been most successful in the *economic* (taxation, pensions), *personal safety* (victims' rights, individual right to self defense, restrictions on bail and release of repeat offenders [especially for sexual and violent crimes]), *suffrage*, *health*, and *gender and racially neutral language* arenas. Slightly lower but still relatively high success rates are observable with regard to civil rights and civil liberties issues. Successes were greater when proposals targeted rights or services for the elderly (e.g., economic, taxation and retirement, health, and some housing) but were less common when they specifically singled out the poor (e.g., housing). (Women make up a disproportionate percentage of each of these groups, the elderly and the poor.) The study shows also that constitutional changes proposed through the formal citizen-initiative process were less likely to be approved than those submitted by state legislatures or constitutional conventions. But many of the defeated citizen-initiated proposals—especially in the health, education, and personal safety areas—proposed government funding or support for private sector ventures.

Susan A. MacManus is affiliated with the University of South Florida.

The author would like to thank the following for their assistance: Dr. Nikki R. Van Hightower, Harris County Treasurer, Houston, TX and Carolyn B. Craske, Graduate Assistant, Department of Public Administration, University of South Florida.

> State constitutions are a font of individual liberties, their protections often extending beyond those required by the Supreme Court's interpretation of Federal law. The legal resolution which has brought federal law to the fore must not be allowed to inhibit the independent protective force of state law—for without it, the full realization of our liberties cannot be guaranteed.
>
> —William J. Brennan, Jr. (1977)
> Associate Justice
> United States Supreme Court

> No aspect of state government has been more severely criticized than state constitutions. Condemned as antiquated, too long and detailed, poorly organized, difficult to amend, and more concerned with restricting state action than facilitating problem solution, constitutions have been under attack in all states for most of this century.
>
> —Mavis Mann Reeves (1982)
> Professor; Coauthor of
> *Pragmatic Federalism*

Throughout American history, state constitutions have been lauded as either the leading agents of change in the battle for more comprehensive civil rights and liberties (Brennan 1977; Sturm and Wright 1975; Welsh and Collins 1981) or as "the drag anchors of state progress . . . permanent cloaks for the protection of special interests and points of view" (Terry Sanford, quoted in Leach 1976, ix; see also Leach 1969). In this paper, we examine this debate in the context of women's rights, focusing primarily on changes in state constitutions over the past decade.

CHANGING DOCUMENTS

Since 1776, the 50 states have operated under no fewer than 146 constitutions. By the end of 1979, a total of 7,563 proposed amendments had been made to operative state constitutions; 4,704 (62%) were adopted (Sturm winter 1982, 74). These changes ranged from alterations in a single section to major rewrites of the entire document. Major changes have often come in flurries, stimulated by federal court rulings (e.g., reapportionment rulings of the 1960s) or social and economic revolutions (the minority rights movements of the 1960s and 1970s, the morality movement of the 1980s). In some cases, state constitutional change lags behind federal constitutional law; in others (such as state ERAs), it leads.

In the 1970s alone, 12 constitutional conventions were held in 10 different states (Browne 1973; Canning 1977; Clark and Clark 1975; Cornwell, Goodman, and Swanson 1975; Dunn 1976; English and Carroll 1982; Goodman, Arseneau, Cornwell, and Swanson 1973; Leach 1973, 1976, 1977; May 1977; Press 1982; Sturm 1979, winter 1982; Yarger 1976). "Practically all new or revised state constitutions provided added protection for individuals against discrimination, although the protection was more extensively racial than gender, or sexual discrimination" (Sturm 1979, 27). However, during the early 1970s some form of an Equal Rights Amendment was inserted into 15 state constitutions: Alaska, Colorado, Connecticut, Hawaii, Illinois, Louisiana, Maryland, Massachusetts, Montana, New Hampshire, New Mexico, Pennsylvania, Texas, Virginia, and Washington. Utah and Wyoming adopted constitutional provisions regarding sex equality near the end of the 19th century (United States Commission on Civil Rights 1981, 1; see also Schlafly 1979).

By the beginning of the 1980s, the pace of state constitutional change had slowed somewhat. Comprehensive revisions emanating from constitutional conventions and commissions were far less common than in the 1970s. Nonetheless, one state adopted a new constitution, its tenth (Georgia in 1982). The District of Columbia's constitutional convention drafted a new constitution in preparation for hoped-for statehood (Sturm and May 1986).

Between 1980 and 1985, there were a significant number of constitutional changes proposed in 45 states, even if there were not many comprehensive rewrites. A total of 708 constitutional changes with statewide applicability were submitted to voters, of which 463 were adopted (65%). (See Sturm winter 1982; Sturm and May

1986.) Thus, even in a "slow" period, changes in state constitutions are common.[1]

With each state "free to adopt its own republican constitution under the federal right of constitutional choices," and with the relatively liberal procedures available for changes, it means that each constitution reflects "the geographic, ethnic, religious, socioeconomic, cultural, and historic" uniqueness of that entity (Elazar 1982, 14). Thus we would expect the constitutions to vary in their coverage of issues and principles affecting women. The premier difficulty lies in defining what is a "women's issue."

WHAT IS A WOMEN'S ISSUE?

We define "women's issues" as those with the potential to impact disproportionately on women due to demographic, socioeconomic, biological, or attitudinal and policy preference patterns. We regard this as a more appropriate way to define women's issues because it permits inclusion of a broader range of policy arenas (e.g., economic and taxation, health, personal safety) than the traditional civil rights and civil liberties and suffrage areas. In a somewhat similar vein, U.S. Representative Pat Schroeder has proposed broadening the definition of women's issues: "Everything we used to call women's issues are really family issues. If you're shortchanging women, you're shortchanging everybody" (Schroeder, quoted in Hannon 1988, 2). Columnist Ellen Goodman (1988) concurs: "Democratic issues just aren't segregated by sex anymore. No longer 'special,' these interests have been recast as family concerns, as economic issues . . . [or issues reaching out] broadly to women in terms of education, health care, child care, jobs" (Goodman 1988, 7G).

We turn now to a review of the success rates of constitutional proposals that might be regarded as "women's issues" that were submitted to the voters of various states during the years 1977 to 1985.[2]

Women's Issues in State Constitutional Changes, 1977-1985

The source of the data for our content analysis of constitutional changes made in the 50 states from 1977 to 1985 is the annual January or February issue of the *National Civil Review*. In it Albert Sturm provides a detailed list of each constitutional change formally submitted for approval, the method by which it was proposed, and its disposition.[3] (The series was discontinued in the 1987 issue, which limits our analysis to the 1977-1985 period.)

We expect to find some unique provisions that are absent from the U.S. Constitution. Judicial scholars Welsh and Collins (1981) tell us, "It is worthy of note that in one or another respect all the texts of individual state constitutions offer some measure of constitutional protection not contained in the text of the U.S. Constitution" (Welsh and Collins 1981, 12). Included among this list are protections of the rights of the handicapped against discriminatory practices (three states), labor organizations and the right to work (nine states), minors and prisoners, environmentalists, and rights governing personal communication and privacy (10 states), euthanasia, the amount of recoverable damages in death or personal injury cases, use of nuclear power, firearms or ammunition, hunting and fishing, revolution, and punishment and rehabilitation.

Welsh and Collins' view of state constitutions as leading agents of change in the area of individual rights is shared by many others, as noted earlier in this paper. Justice Brennan says it well: "The notion that state constitutional provisions were adopted to mirror the federal Bill of Rights [has been put to rest]. The lesson of history is otherwise; indeed, the drafters of the federal Bill of Rights drew upon corresponding provisions in the various state constitutions. Prior to the adoption of the federal constitution, each of the rights eventually recognized in the federal Bill of Rights had previously been protected in one or more state constitutions" (Brennan 1977, 501). Today, state constitutions are also unique in their detailing of the rights of individuals and groups to benefits in various substantive policy arenas.

Substantive Areas of Change

The substantive areas that have received the most attention from scholars studying women's rights are those labeled "Bill of Rights" and "Suffrage and Elections." We, however, extend our analysis to include economic and taxation, personal safety, health, housing, and transportation issues, especially as they affect the poor and elderly (disproportionately women). We focus on substantive rather than procedural changes (amendment processes).

Our substantive categories consist of Economic and Taxation, Personal Safety (protection against violent crimes, criminals, and repeat offenders; right of self-defense), Housing, Health, Civil Rights and Civil Liberties (including ERAs), Education, Suffrage, and Language (gender and race neutral). Our results show the following breakdown by category of the 126 women's issue constitutional changes submitted between 1977 and 1985: Economic and Taxation (28%); Personal Safety (22%); Civil Rights and Civil Liberties (18%); Language (gender and race neutral) (9%); Health (3%); Housing (8%); Education (4%); and Suffrage (3%).[4] Of these 126 issues, 28 failed (22%). (See Table 1.) Of the failures, only four bore gender-related language (Florida ERA, 1978; Iowa ERA, 1980; Maine ERA, 1982; New Hampshire gender-neutral language, 1980).

Only 16 of the 126 issues specifically mentioned sex or gender (limit on public funding of abortion but not on preventing death of a pregnant woman or of her unborn child in a life-threatening situation, Colorado, 1984; "No person will be deprived of any right because of sex," Florida, 1978; instatement of gender-neutral language, Georgia, 1981; prohibition of discrimination in public educational institutions on the basis of sex, Hawaii, 1978; removal of language applicable only to persons of one sex, Hawaii, 1978; elimination of language restricting offices that women can hold and elections in which women can vote, Idaho, 1982; ERA, Iowa, 1980; prohibition against denial or abridgement of equality under the law because of sex, Maine, 1982; deletion of requirement that state librarian be a woman, Mississippi, 1978; deletion of requirement for registration of the separate property of married women, Nevada, 1978; elimination of restrictions on female elector eligibil-

TABLE 1. Summary of State Constitutional Changes Affecting Women's Issues, 1977-1985, by Issue Area, Method of Proposal, and Success Rate

Issue	% of Proposals (n=126)	METHOD OF PROPOSAL				% Success (n=101)
		Legis. (n=103)	Init. (n=12)	Const Conv. (n=10)	Rev. Conv. (n=1)	
Economic & Taxation	28%	29%	33%	-	-	85%
Personal Safety	22%	23%	33%	-	-	89%
Civil Rights/ Civil Liberties	18%	17%	17%	30%	1%	75%
Language (Gender & Race Neutral)	9%	8%	-	20% 10% Rev.	-	91%
Health	8%	7%	-	30%	-	80%
Housing	8%	8%	8%	-	-	56%
Education	4%	4%	8%	-	-	20%
Suffrage	3%	3%	-	10%	100%	100%
TOTALS	100%	99%*	99%*	100%	101%*	

*Note: Figures may not add to 100% due to rounding.

Source: Abstracted from annual articles by Albert Sturm (and various coauthors in the January or February issue of the *National Civic Review*. The authors of this article identified changes that were related to women's issues and classified them by type of issue.

ity for office, Nevada, 1978; elimination of masculine language, New Hampshire, 1980; removal of prohibitions against women working in underground mines, Utah, 1980; removal of gender-specific terminology, Wisconsin, 1982; permission for legislature to locate a penitentiary for women somewhere in the state, Wyoming, 1978; repeal of prohibition of females from working in the mines, Wyoming, 1978). In summary, most of the amendments specifically mentioning gender fall under the Civil Rights and Civil Liberties or Language classifications. The success rate was higher for Language (91%) than Civil Rights and Civil Liberties amendments (75%).

Of course, some of the issues that passed may not be regarded by feminists as pro-women (e.g., Colorado's 1984 limit on public funding of abortion). But we really do not know how women in Colorado voted on the issue. Without exit polls in each state it is difficult to make definitive statements about the cohesiveness of the women's vote, especially on many other issues that are not traditionally viewed as women's issues.

More frequent than mention of gender is the targeting of constitutional protections, rights, and benefits to the elderly. A review of the 126 changes submitted shows that 21 specifically singled out the elderly. Most of these provided tax benefits in the form of higher homestead exemptions (Arizona, 1980; Georgia, 1980; New Jersey, 1980; Texas, 1970; West Virginia, 1980, 1982). Several dealt with pension and retirement benefit transfers to survivors (Nebraska, 1978; Pennsylvania, 1984). Others delineated state responsibility for health, transportation, security, housing, and voting accessibility for the elderly (Hawaii, 1978; New Hampshire, 1984; New Jersey, 1981; Oregon, 1978, 1980, 1982; Texas, 1982). Since women are a much larger proportion of the elderly population, the success of such legislation should be viewed positively by women's rights advocates.

The rising incidence of violent and sexual crimes (often related), along with increasingly higher recidivism rates among criminals, has meant that the right of self-defense (including the right to bear arms), the right to deny bail to repeat offenders, and the right to impose tougher incarceration restrictions are getting more support among women now than in the past. We labeled these as Personal

Safety issues. There were a number of these placed before voters for approval in the 1977-1985 time period, the bulk of which passed. Voters in many states approved limiting bail, especially for those accused of violent crimes (Arizona, 1982; Colorado, 1982; Illinois, 1982; Michigan, 1978; Nebraska [provided that certain sexual crimes shall be nonbailable], 1978; Nevada, 1980; New Mexico, 1980; Rhode Island, 1984; Texas, 1977; Vermont, 1982; Wisconsin, 1981). Maximum sentencing was approved in Idaho and in Oklahoma in 1978. Compensation for victims of crimes was endorsed by voters in California (1982) and Georgia (1978). And the right to bear arms was given additional constitutional emphasis in Idaho (1978), Nevada (1982), New Hampshire (1982), and North Dakota (1984).

Another group of issues targeted constitutional protection and provisions for the poor in a variety of areas, primarily housing and welfare. Here the success rate was not as uniform. For example, government support for low-income housing was twice endorsed in Oregon (1978, 1980) but failed in California (1980) and Ohio (1977, 1980). Exemption of food and drugs from state sales taxes also met with mixed results (Arkansas, 1978—failed; Nevada, 1980—passed; Nevada, 1982—failed; Nevada, 1984—passed). There was only one instance of a welfare-to-the-needy provision (Texas, 1982—passed).

In general, then, constitutional protections and provisions specifically targeting the poor were not as likely to be approved as those aimed at wider recipient groups. From the perspective of women's rights advocates, this finding is not cause for joy—or for views of state constitutions as leading agents of change—since the overwhelming majority of the poor are women and children.

Strictly family- or child-oriented constitutional changes were not common (although, as U.S. Representative Schroeder notes, every women's issue is really a family issue). Ironically, most of these changes had to do with making dissolution of the family easier—e.g., Nevada's 1978 provision to delineate more clearly the property rights of married women (passed), South Carolina's 1978 reduction of the period of continuous separation (from three years to one) as an allowed ground for divorce (passed), Texas' 1980 authorization for spouses to agree that income or property arising from separate property is to be separate (rather than community) property (passed). Only one dealt specifically with child support: Texas (1982) authorized the legislature to provide for the garnishment of wages to enforce court-ordered child support payments (passed). Another eliminated the prohibition against interracial marriages (Tennessee, 1978).

Support for government financing or regulation of health services and facilities (of which the elderly and youth are disproportionately heavy users) was mixed. Such proposals were supported in Georgia (1978), Hawaii (1978), New Jersey (1981), and Texas (1982, 1985) but were defeated in Arizona (1982) and Idaho (1978, 1980). Most often, defeat occurred when a proposal called for public support for or regulation of religious or private firms. This same debate prevailed in the education area, where proposals for state funding and support for private schools was consistently defeated (California, 1982; Massachusetts, 1982; Michigan, 1978; North Carolina, 1982).

A few of the other education-related provisions eliminated racially discriminatory language (Oklahoma, 1978; Tennessee, 1978; both passed). One dealt with school prayer (West Virginia, 1984); it also passed.

Success Rates by Method of Proposal

The success rate of constitutional changes varied by the type of method used to propose it. The data show that changes submitted by state legislatures had the highest success rate (83%), followed closely by convention-initiated changes (80%). Citizen-drafted changes (initiatives and Florida's revision commission) fared less well (with 50% and 0% success rates respectively). These findings are consistent with those of other scholars (e.g., Press 1982; Sturm and May 1986). Press (1982, 111) suggests that the reason citizen-initiated proposals are less successful is that they tend to yield radical constitutional changes—"radical in that [they have] a marked influence in reshaping current policy and operations." "More common," he notes, "are constitutional changes that ratify battles already won, or changes that aid in bringing to a successful conclusion political battles almost won" (Press 1982, 110).

This suggests that, more often than not, state constitutional changes may lag behind societal changes. But not always: Our analysis of state constitutional changes between 1977 and 1985 suggests that, insofar as the treatment of women's issues goes, the lag may be greater in the civil rights and civil liberties arenas than in substantive policy areas such as economic, health, welfare, and housing.[5] Specifically, insertion of amendments expressly prohibiting discrimination on the basis of race, gender, religious belief, or mental or physical condition and amendments assuring individual right to privacy have lagged behind federal, state, and local statutes and practices.

CONCLUSION

Our analysis of the constitutional changes related to women's issues (those that disproportionately impact on women as a consequence of demographic, socioeconomic, biological, or attitudinal patterns) between 1977 and 1985 shows that state constitutions are both leading and lagging agents of change in comparison with the U.S. Constitution and with each other. We should be encouraged by their economic, health, and personal safety protections and provisions but less so by their mixed results with regard to extension of equal civil rights and liberties and to direct provisions for care of the poor. Our analyses confirm what Justice Louis Brandeis observed over a half-century ago: "A single courageous state may, if its citizens choose, serve as a laboratory and try moral, social and economic experiments" (quoted in Welsh and Collins 1981, 7). But it also shows that some states have longer histories of boldness than others, reflecting cultural, socioeconomic, and political differences in their constituencies.

While women's rights advocates may be somewhat inclined to view some state constitutions as "drag anchors" insofar as proposed change that specifically mentions gender-equality, they should take heart and view most constitutions as positive agents of change, for the most part bettering the economic and social policy conditions enjoyed by women. While constitutional change is but the first step down the long road toward equality, it is nonetheless a giant one, and one that often begins (and ends) at the state rather than the federal level.

NOTES

1. Throughout the 50 states, there are four commonly used methods of initiating change (Dye 1988, 36):

a. *Legislative proposal*: Amendments are passed by the state legislature and then submitted to the voters for approval in a referendum (used by all states, although in Delaware voter approval is not required).
b. *Popular initiative*: A specific number of voters petition to get a constitutional amendment on the ballot for approval by the voters in a referendum (Alaska, Arizona, California, Colorado, Florida, Illinois, Massachusetts, Michigan, Missouri, Montana, Nebraska, Nevada, North Dakota, Ohio, Oklahoma, Oregon, and South Dakota).
c. *Constitutional Convention*: Legislatures submit to the voters a proposal for calling a constitutional convention, and, if voters approve, a convention convenes, draws up constitutional revisions, and submits them again for approval by the voters in a referendum (41 states—see Sturm 1987). There are 14 states that require periodic submission to the voters of the question of calling a constitutional convention: eight states every 20 years (Connecticut, Illinois, Maryland, Missouri, Montana, New York, Ohio, and Oklahoma), four states every 10 years (Arkansas, Iowa, New Hampshire, and Rhode Island), one every 16 years (Michigan), and one every nine years (Hawaii).
d. *Constitutional Commission*: Commissions are created by the legislature to study the constitution and recommend changes to the state legislature. In the state of Florida, the recommendations of the commission are submitted directly to the voters in a referendum.

2. We recognize, of course, that women often differ considerably in their public policy preferences due to variances in age, race or ethnicity, income, education, regional location, ideology, and political party affiliation (Boles 1979; Boneparth and Stoper 1988; Hannon 1988; Poole and Ziegler 1985; Schlafly 1977).

3. While the Sturm data may legitimately be criticized for its lack of detail in delineating each amendment's potential impact on women, it is still the most comprehensive longitudinal data set on state constititional amendment proposals and adoptions.

4. A detailed state-by-state listing of these proposed amendments is available from the authors upon request.

5. It is important to note that constitutional guarantees are but one step toward the achievement of equality. Implementation is an equally important, and often

difficult, next step in the policy process. See MacManus and Van Hightower (forthcoming), "The Limits of State Constituitional Guarantees: Lessons From Efforts to Implement Domestic Violence and Sexual Assault Policies."

REFERENCES

Boles, Janet. 1979. *The Politics of the Equal Rights Amendment*. New York: Longman.

Boneparth, Ellen, and Emily Stoper, eds. 1988. *Women, Power, and Policy*, 2nd ed. New York: Pergamon Press.

Brennan, William J., Jr. January 1977. "State Constitutions and the Protection of Individual Rights." *Harvard Law Review* 90:489-504.

Browne, Cynthia E. 1973. *State Constitutional Conventions: From Independence to the Completion of the Present Union 1776-1959: A Bibliography*. Westport, CT: Greenwood Press.

Canning, Bonnie. 1977. *State Constitutional Conventions, Revisions and Amendments, 1959-1976: A Bibliography*. Westport, CT: Greenwood Press.

Clark, Cal, and Janet Clark. 1975. "The Impact of Party and Electoral Systems on Political Conflict in State Constitutional Conventions." *Western Political Quarterly* 28:700-711.

Cornwell, Elmer E., Jr., Jay S. Goodman, and Wayne R. Swanson. 1975. *State Constitutional Conventions: The Politics of the Revision Process in Seven States*. New York: Praeger.

Dunn, Charles. January 1976. "Comparative Partisan and Group Voting Behavior in Constitutional Conventions: A Research Note." *American Politics Quarterly* 4:115-120.

Dye, Thomas R. 1988. *Politics in States and Communities*, 6th ed. Englewood Cliffs, NJ: Prentice-Hall.

Elazar, Daniel J. Winter 1982. "The Principles and Traditions Underlying State Constitutions." *Publius* 12:11-26.

English, Arthur, and John J. Carroll. May 1982. "Constitutional Reform in Arkansas: The 1979-1980 Convention." *National Civic Review* 71:240-250, 267.

Goodman, Ellen. "Political Issues Aren't Segregated by Sex Anymore." *The Houston Post*, 24 July 1988.

Goodman, Jay S., Robert Arseneau, Elmer E. Cornwell, Jr., and Wayne R. Swanson. 1973. "Public Responses to State Constitutional Revision." *American Journal of Political Science* 17:571-596.

Hannon, Sharron. January-February 1988. "Women and the '88 Elections." *Southern Changes* 10:1-3.

Leach, Richard H. 1969. *Compacts of Antiquity: State Constitutions*. Atlanta: Southern Newspaper Publishers Association Foundation.

Leach, Richard H. 1973. Introduction. In *State Constitutional Conventions: From*

Independence to the Completion of the Present Union 1776-1959: A Bibliography, Cynthia E. Brown. Westport, CT: Greenwood Press.

Leach, Richard H. 1976. Introduction. In *State Constitutional Conventions, 1959-1975: A Bibliography*, ed. Susan Rice Yarger. Westport, CT: Greenwood Press.

Leach, Richard H. 1977. A Quiet Revolution: 1933-1976. *Book of the States, 1975-76*. Lexington, KY: Council of State Governments.

May, Janice C. Winter 1977. "The Purposes of American State Constitutions." *Publius* 12:27-44.

Poole, Keith T., and L. Harmon Zeigler. 1985. *Women, Public Opinion, and Politics: The Changing Political Attitudes of American Women*. New York: Longman.

Press, Charles. Winter 1982. "Assessing the Policy and Operational Implications of State Constitutional Change." *Publius* 12:99-111.

Reeves, Mavis Mann. Spring 1982. "Look Again at State Capacity: The Old Gray Mare Ain't What She Used to Be." *American Review of Public Administration* 16:74-88.

Schlafly, Phyllis. 1977. *The Power of the Positive Woman*. New Rochelle, NY: Arlington House.

Schlafly, Phyllis. Summer 1979. "The Effect of Equal Rights Amendments in State Constitutions." *Policy Review* 9:55-84.

Sturm, Albert L. 1978. State Constitutions and Constitutional Revision, 1976-77. *Book of the States, 1978-79*. Lexington, KY: Council of State Governments.

Sturm, Albert L. 1979. "State Constitutional Conventions During the 1970s." *State Government* 52:24-30.

Sturm, Albert L. January 1980. "State Constitutional Developments During 1979 and the 1970s." *National Civic Review* 69:33-40.

Sturm, Albert L. January 1981. "State Constitutional Developments During 1980." *National Civic Review* 70:22-36.

Sturm, Albert L. January 1982. "State Constitutional Developments During 1981." *National Civic Review* 71:28-32.

Sturm, Albert L. Winter 1982. "The Development of American State Constitutions." *Publius* 12:57-98.

Sturm, Albert L. January 1983. "State Constitutional Developments During 1982." *National Civic Review* 72:35-50.

Sturm, Albert L. January 1984. "State Constitutional Developments During 1983." *National Civic Review* 73:24-30.

Sturm, Albert L. January-February 1986. "State Constitutional Developments During 1985." *National Civic Review* 75:35-39.

Sturm, Albert L., and Janice C. May. 1986. State Constitutions and Constitutional Revision: 1984-85. *The Book of the States, 1986-87*. Lexington, KY: Council of State Governments.

Sturm, Albert L., and Kaye M. Wright. 1975. "Civil Liberties in Revised State Constitutions." *Policy Studies Journal* 4:162-167.

Sturm, Albert L., and Kaye M. Wright. 1978. "State Constitutional Developments During 1977." *National Civic Review* 67:31-36.

United States Commission on Civil Rights. 1981. *The Equal Rights Amendment: Guaranteeing Equal Rights for Women Under the Constitution*. Washington, D.C.: U.S. Government Printing Office.

Welsh, Robert, and Ronald K. L. Collins. September-October 1981. "Taking State Constitutions Seriously." *The Center Magazine* 14:6-35.

Yarger, Susan Rice. 1976. *State Constitutional Conventions, 1959-1975: A Bibliography*. Westport, CT: Greenwood Press.